The Journey into Self

ALSO BY CHARLES LEVITON , EdD
PATTI LEVITON, MA

More Fully Human
The Struggle To Be Me – With You

There is No Bad Truth
The Search for Self

The Miracle of Words

The Conflict Between Us is the Conflict Within Me

Inner Peace – Outward Power
Guided Imagery to Use with the 12 Steps to Recovery

The Journey into Self

How to Use Guided Imagery to
Empower Your Life and Heal
Physically and Emotionally

Charles D. Leviton, EdD,
and Patti Leviton, MA

Order this book online at www.trafford.com
or email orders@trafford.com

Most Trafford titles are also available at major online book retailers.

Printed in the United States of America.

ISBN: 978-1-4269-6746-7 (sc)
ISBN: 978-1-4269-6747-4 (e)

Trafford rev. 06/27/2011

 www.trafford.com

North America & International
toll-free: 1 888 232 4444 (USA & Canada)
phone: 250 383 6864 ✦ fax: 812 355 4082

I've had the pleasure of knowing Patti & Chuck Leviton for many years now, and the honor of attending several of their healing and guided imagery workshops and certification programs. I can say from personal experience that both Chuck & Patti are masters in the healing arts.

I have witnessed seemingly miraculous emotional healings and awakenings take place during their guided imagery sessions. *The Journey Into Self* is the culmination (so far!) of their experience, knowledge and wisdom.

I use all of their practices and techniques, to one degree or another, in my own self and group healing work; I can attest to their power and effectiveness.

In a material world seemingly designed to keep us physically and emotionally disempowered and convinced that healing can take place only through the intervention of the pharmaceutical industry, here is a book that returns the power to heal back into our hands.

The Journey Into Self is filled with simple techniques that can produce profound results, told in a clear and to-the-point style, yet also filled with the deep insight and loving compassion of both Patti & Chuck. *Physician, heal thyself!* - And now the same can be said to each of us.

Read this book and be grateful.

Namaste,
Bradley Rand Smith
Reiki practitioner, meditation & self-healing facilitator, author, playwright, *Johnny Got His Gun*

We dedicate this book to all the students and graduates
of our Guided Imagery Certification Program.
Your eagerness to learn and refine your skills in
this powerful modality of healing made this book possible.

"The Levitons provide unique insight and depth examining the clinical value of guided imagery, offering a host of practices and approaches that integrate traditional psychodynamic work with Jungian symbology and the most current thinking about the mind-body connection. Rich in clinical example and practice wisdom, this book is an excellent addition to the library of any practitioner with an interest in this wonderful therapeutic tool."

Belleruth Naparstek, Author of *Invisible Heroes: Survivors of Trauma & How They Heal* and creator of the Health Journeys guided imagery audio series

"A fascinating compilation of the Leviton's years of expertise and experience. A treasure trove of insightful gifts for all interested in the magic of guided imagery - professional and layperson alike. Read this book and allow your world to be transformed and healed."

Charlotte Reznick PhD, Author of *The Power of Your Child's Imagination: How to Transform Stress and Anxiety into Joy and Success*

CONTENTS

PREFACE

WHY THIS BOOK

This book is entitled: The Journey into Self – to empower your life and heal physically and emotionally.

Guided Imagery IS the answer!

About fifteen years ago we started a company called Synergy Seminars and created a program to certify people to become Guided Imagery Therapists. We are one of just a hand full of national programs that advertise and provide this type of training. Also, we are one of just a few that will train laypersons, as well as professionals in the health care field.

In traveling the country, attending conferences and doing seminars, we have had the privilege of meeting thousands of people who knew of guided imagery, by one name or another, and have experienced it many times, even using it with clients or friends. When questioned about where they learned it, most laughed and said they'd had no formal training, didn't even know such training existed, or had just learned by having the experience themselves. They found it to be very relaxing, and used the technique with clients.

Many of these people have decided to be certified with us, and we have often been told that even people who felt very comfortable using guided imagery on a consistent basis report that, *I had no idea of the depth and power of imagery for resolving past traumas, healing physical illness and correcting false belief systems that were controlling my life. I just used it for general relaxation or stress reduction and providing positive affirmations.* All good uses, by the way, but they are barely scratching the surface of possibilities.

Professional therapists with years of personal therapy behind them have shared with us, *I've worked on this issue for years and felt I had come to a place of understanding and healing a long time ago, but I've never had the depth of healing and change that I've experienced with your imagery.*

In creating this certification program and presenting our unique approach called IntraPersonal Imagery, one of our strongest motivations was to teach people by experiencing guided imagery themselves. Anyone who hasn't experienced imagery's powerful access to the unconscious for life changing results will be limited in their ability to take clients to that place of wisdom within.

It is safe to say that most, if not all of our graduates, feel there has been a significant change in every aspect of their personal lives as a result of this training. The second motivation is to provide the skills, theory and structure to do imagery well, with a sense of confidence and experience necessary to work with clients on any level that is required.

But foremost, there is an incredible mind-body connection, and through imagery, we can not only heal emotionally, but physically. In changing belief systems and literally 'talking' to any imbalance or health issue, we can give back to the body the permission to heal. The body knows exactly how to maintain good health, if we'll just get out of our own way.

This book is essentially an expanded version of our certification program, teaching the history and background of imagery and how it connects with dreams and mythology, providing psychological theory and values for living a rich and balanced life. We provide our students with the opportunity to experience twelve group imageries that are geared to personal growth and insight, plus three demonstrations of a one-on-one imagery and how it differs from the group experience.

The major difference between group and one-on-one imagery is simple. In the group imagery, you can use a prepared script to provide a complete experience for any number of people at the same time. In facilitating group imageries in our seminars, everyone experiences the adventure silently. We allow time after the experience for participants to write down what they saw and felt, and then open a group discussion for individuals to share. This dialogue can provide new insights and help interpret the messages and the true meaning of the imagery. Analyzing the experience, similar to analyzing a dream, can bring profound new information.

Since we are told through modern research that the brain cannot distinguish between what's real and what's imagined, we can re-frame past traumas, change belief systems and bring about physical healing through the journey of our imaginations.

In group imagery, even though everyone all heard the same script, each person will have their own private experience. For instance, if a group of ten people are asked to see a horse, they would all see a very unique horse, with various sizes, colors, personalities and environments. Understanding the symbolism of perhaps a large, powerful horse in an open meadow versus a skittish animal in a small corral could provide insight into where the listener is in their life right now.

One-on-one imagery is very different, in that after you have relaxed the client and put them in a place of peace, perhaps a meadow or at the beach, the therapist and client can then begin a dialogue with each other. Using the example of a horse, the therapist could ask, "Describe the horse to me", and then follow the client as the story unfolds.

If you've ever searched the internet looking for guided imagery, you're probably aware that there are thousands of people and organizations listed offering some type of guided imagery service. What they all call imagery is probably as varied in approach and method as each of the people offering it. We often say to our clients, there is no wrong way to do imagery and whatever you see or experience is personal to you and not to be judged. We also don't choose to judge others who are providing the services of imagery or their approach. We don't wish to compare ourselves and our work to others.

This book is designed to share our personal approach, what we call IntraPersonal Imagery; the essence of what we teach in our certification program. IntraPersonal Imagery is our process of guided imagery, culled and refined for over 40 years.

If you are now using guided imagery or are interested in learning to use it as a complementary tool in your work as any type of health practitioner, both holistic and allopathic, this book can be a great service to you. We will offer you a complete tool box of ideas and approaches that will enable you to create your own individual imageries, or how to use scripts written by others and get the best results in helping clients.

One of the most important features of this book is that we will provide you with a basic structure that can be used with any imagery, whether it's a group experience or one-on-one. In the one-on-one session, even though you are following the client, we will give you the framework so that you are always aware of the goals and purpose of your imagery and provide you with certain tools you can use to arrive at the best destination for the client. With this basic structure as support, you can create your own imageries for any client and any situation.

This is a book for the polarized world of today; a world that is caught up in all the power struggles that separate and divide us. Teaching the uses of guided imagery, with its instant access to the unconscious, we can uncover the false belief systems, unfinished business of the past and explore the real reasons for this polarization in our personal lives, as well as on our planet.

From discovering the true issues that need attention in your life, to a final resolution of making peace with personal pain, this book will provide theory and direction in a simple and straightforward approach. With both theories and communication skills, we will provide a new and gentle approach for breaking down defenses, knowing and expressing your own truth. This approach expresses an openness to encouraging change in others by changing the way you present and change yourself.

In addition, as you help others by using imagery to explore the unfinished issues from the past found in the unconscious mind, you will find yourself using these same skills and wisdom in your everyday exchanges with others.

This is a handbook for creating and using the powerful and mystical techniques of guided imagery to heal both physical and emotional issues, but it is also a handbook for living a balanced life of gentleness, love, tolerance and understanding; a world that doesn't judge character, but values differences.

It is our hope that this introduction has given you some insight as to how this book can be a value to increase your knowledge of the wonderful, healing, mystical, sometimes miraculous, world of guided imagery.

INTRODUCTION

WE ARE WHAT WE THINK

We are intrigued and pleased with the current increase in scientific studies on the mind-body connection. The research of biochemists such as Dr. Candace Pert is proving that there is a connection between our thoughts, emotions, even the words we speak, and our physiology. Her fascinating work is substantiating that feelings can stimulate certain hormones and chemicals in the body that can enhance or suppress the immune system; that a negative attitude, for example, can literally lower metabolism. No wonder that dieting never works when we're depressed!

We believe, therefore, that the first step to a more holistic lifestyle begins with being AWARE. Just by being aware of our thoughts, our state of mind, our attitudes, we can make a subtle shift. The body, an obedient and faithful servant, is listening.

With both of us growing up in Chicago, in the fall season our families would start stocking the medicine cabinets with cold pills and aspirin The flu season would soon be upon us. Alas, self-fulfilling prophecy, our bodies obeyed, and sure enough, we would have a bout with the flu. The body was providing what we asked for and expected.

Similarly, as we indulge in a marvelous hot fudge sundae, we often say, "I'm going to gain ten pounds!" And we do. The body is always listening. Think about all the negative and often erroneous information we 'feed' our bodies on a daily basis. Review your belief systems for the truth you tell your body. Think about the dialogue, the positive as well as the negative things you convey to yourself. What is your belief about your health? What do you tell yourself about diet?

We have the power to control our thoughts, adjust our attitudes, our outlook, and slowly, the body is given the permission to heal. We can give the body freedom to mend and perform all the functions of health in perfection. This indeed is a continual process of our own self talk. By affirmation, whether it is through our thoughts or our words, or incorporating the powerful modality of guided imagery, the body will obey in health.

The second step in this journey of health is BELIEF. Modern science is continually baffled by the phenomenon of the placebo effect. When we believe that a certain procedure or medication will be effective, it will. Increasing the efficacy by 60 to 70%, we believe our positive self talk to the body is working.

Decades ago, during the Vietnam conflict, unprepared for the enormity of the conflict, medics found themselves too often tending to the severely wounded with no morphine. Time after time, they would administer an IV saline solution, the only thing they had, telling the soldiers that it was morphine and that their pain would soon subside. Within a short time, the pain was alleviated. How? Was it their belief that it was morphine that tricked the body into producing the chemicals, the endorphins, necessary to block pain? Lab reports taken from these soldiers who had been given only saline, but with the understanding that it was morphine, revealed there was morphine in the blood. Where did it come from? The body was listening.

Wherever your healing journey takes you, be aware of your self talk. Do you believe in the treatment, what is your belief system about each particular modality? If you believe and have confidence, the body hears this and will respond in a positive way. If you are fearful and apprehensive, the body likewise will react in a negative way.

And the third step in the process is REMEMBERED WELLNESS. As researched by Dr. Herbert Benson, Harvard University Medical School, when we visualize or think about our bodies in health, remembering a time when we felt our bodies were the strongest and healthiest, certain hormones and chemicals are literally secreted to replicate that good health. Time and again, in our private practice, we use this technique with clients to promote healing. As they imagine and remember themselves in perfect health, their bodies obey.

Right now, think about a time when you felt the best, when you felt you were the healthiest. It could be last week, last year, or twenty years ago. Close your eyes and literally see yourself as that strong, perfect you. Feel the balance, the strength. Now, throughout your day, continue to think about that healthy you. The body is listening. Research has proven that just by focusing and thinking about yourself in health enhances the immune system. By doing a simple saliva test, scientists are proving that the immunoglobulin A, which is a precursor in the stimulation of the immune system, increases, proving a powerful mind-body connection.

Your journey to a more holistic lifestyle begins with being AWARE. Your very thoughts and attitudes can greatly affect your health, positively or negatively. It's your choice. Then add BELIEF, the strong commitment that what you are doing is in the best interest of your health and well being. And, lastly, focus on the healthy aspect of you, the REMEMBERED WELLNESS of when you felt the strongest and healthiest. Your body is a faithful obedient servant that will respond.

And so, we present this book to you in the hopes you will find these tools helpful in creating, facilitating and interpreting guided imagery. With an AWARENESS of the power of this modality, and the BELIEF in its efficacy to heal, both physically and emotionally, the possibilities are endless. And with that REMEMERED WELLNESS, imagery can be a tool to bring a healthy balance and peace to ourselves, our community, our nation, our planet.

In *The Spontaneous Healing of Belief,* Gregg Braden states that, *It only takes the square root of one percent of a population to begin a change. This calculation represents only the minimum needed to begin the process. The more people involved in feeling peace, the faster the effect is created.*

Let there be peace on earth and let it begin with me.

CHAPTER ONE

HISTORY OF GUIDED IMAGERY

Guided imagery is as old as psychotherapy itself. However, as a relatively new approach in the United States, it is experiencing a real wave of respect, and is part of the cutting edge in the new mind-body medical model. There are many names for this process: visualizations, mental imagery, guided affective imagery, active imagination, and interactive guided imagery. We call our approach IntraPersonal Imagery.

For the first time in history, Western-styled allopathic medicine is embracing alternative healing methods, such as yoga, meditation, and guided imagery. Major universities and hospital centers are combining imagery with traditional healing practices as an integral tool in healing catastrophic illness, as well as quicker recovery from surgical procedures.

Pioneers in the field such as Bernie Siegel, MD and O. Carl Simonton, MD, both best selling authors, have been successfully utilizing guided imagery for over thirty years in the treatment of cancer. The American Society of Colon and Rectal Surgeons report that, *Guided imagery, a low-tech relaxation technique, reduced pain and anxiety after colorectal surgery, helping people heal better and faster.*

As stated in *Spontaneous Evolution*, Bruce Lipton's most recent book, *One third of all illnesses heal via the magic of the placebo.* And, through guided imagery, we can give the body these messages of healing and a return to wellness.

Modern science has grappled with the phenomenon of the placebo for decades. Blind studies and double-blind studies continually baffle technicians as to why almost 60% of all research reveals a physical relief using imaginary medication. This percentage has steadily increased over the years. Possibly this escalation has some relationship to our ever growing awareness of the mind-body connection. If there is a true confidence in the drug or procedure, it will work. Likewise, in guided imagery – if there are positive affirmations to the body – it will heal.

In the 1980's there was a gentleman in his mid-thirties. He had been battling lung cancer for almost two years. He was invited to take part in a research study for FDA approval of Laetrile, a new drug hailed to be the cure for cancer. He had nothing to lose since at this point in his journey, the doctors had given him about two months to live. With extreme optimism, he agreed, and after two months of supervised treatments, his symptoms began to subside. His belief in the efficacy of the drug was reinforced and within one year his cancer was in remission. Laetrile was a wonder drug.

His health was restored. This miraculous treatment had saved his life. Years later, research continued to evaluate Laetrile, and concluded, contrary to just a handful of isolated positive responses to the medication, it was not the wonder drug it was originally thought to be. The FDA declined approval. Within a few short months of reading this information in his morning newspaper, our gentleman was once again diagnosed with lung cancer. His cancer had returned and within six months, he died.

Was it the belief in the drug that had cured him? Did his belief change after so many years of remission? Did learning that the treatment was really a failure cause his cancer to return? Our scientists are challenged by these questions as they continually report positive symptom relief from blind study patients using only a placebo. Laetrile was certainly not a placebo drug, a sugar pill, but when our faith in the effectiveness of any medication is dashed, our bodies truly listen. If we believe in the success of a drug, our bodies listen, too.

We are told there is not a drug in the pharmacy that the body cannot replicate itself. The body has the ability to create all the chemicals necessary for healing and the maintenance of good health. Could it be that we should embrace medicine as a jump start to give our incredible anatomy the permission to heal itself? A drug could be introduced into our system as a reminder of what the body needs to produce itself to heal, maintain and regulate. Once the body is aware of this assistance from a pharmaceutical, and with the belief in the efficacy of the drug, the healing can begin. Gradually, the body has permission to balance and regain strength on its own.

Imagery can be extremely effective with clients going through chemotherapy. By giving the body permission to use all the chemicals being injected into the system to heal and strengthen the immune system, we can further instruct the body to flush out those parts of the medication that are harmful and toxic. Amazingly, clients listening to guided imagery during treatment consistently report fewer symptoms of nausea, fatigue and hair loss.

There was an incredible study done years ago in Minneapolis. We first heard about the research on a video produced and narrated by Bill Moyers, *Healing and the Mind*. A young girl by the name of Marette was battling a chronic situation of lupus. Taking high levels of steroids relieved her symptoms and kept the disease in check, however, the side effects of the drug were staggering. Gradually, over the course of almost five years, the amount of steroids necessary to alleviate the symptoms of the disease, and the symptoms of the drug itself, increased to life threatening dosages. At the rate of this escalated usage, her prognosis was poor.

Dr. Karen Olness, Marette's doctor, was extremely concerned, and being sensitive to the mind-body connection, began a phenomenal experiment. Knowing that any further increase in Marette's medication could prove fatal, Dr. Olness consulted with Dr. Robert Ader, researcher and expert in the classic conditioned response. As the sense of taste and smell are the most easily conditioned, together the two doctors prescribed the addition of two new medicines to Marette's current protocol of chemotherapy called cytosine.

First Marette was instructed to take a tablespoon of cod liver oil when the cytosine was being administered. Additionally, she was told to smell the fragrance of an essential oil of rose petals. Whenever Marette was given the cytosine, her sense of taste and her sense of smell were simultaneously stimulated. Her body was being conditioned to now associate the efficacy of the drug with roses and cod liver oil.

By the end of three months, Dr. Olness decreased the dosage of cytosine by one-quarter, but continued the sensory stimulation. To everyone's amazement, Marette experienced no change. The disease was staying at bay, even with a decrease in medication. Continuing this protocol, at the end of six months, the chemotherapy was reduced further. And again, Marette's symptoms of lupus stayed in check, now with only half the medication.

At the end of one year, the amount of cytosine was again decreased to only a quarter of her original dosage. With this reduction in the drug, slowly Marette's side effects started to disappear. Continuing the process of taking cod liver oil and smelling the rose oil, after three years, Marette's lupus can now be controlled with a far less toxic drug.

Slowly, Marette gave her body the permission to manufacture most of the chemicals on its own to restore health. Eventually, graduating to a much milder medication, her prognosis is wonderful and she continues to smell the roses.

Dr. Olness was using the classic conditioning technique pioneered by Pavlov. Dr. Pavlov was famous for his experiments with dogs, pairing the sight of food with the sound of a bell. The hungry dogs would begin to salivate at the sight of the food in anticipation of being fed. Eventually, the sound of the bell alone caused salivation without the food. Similarly, Marette's body associated the taste and smell with the strong dosage of medication she began with. Slowly, the toxic medication decreased, but the body response remained the same.

One of our own clients by the name of Sophia, shared with us her diagnosis of lupus, almost twenty years ago, and that she was controlling her disease with a steroid called prednisone, as much as 80 milligrams daily. Like Marette's story, the drug alleviated the sometimes excruciating arthritic pain of lupus. However, slowly the side effects of the steroids were outweighing the benefits. In addition to disorientation, thinning of the skin and hair loss, commonly associated with prednisone, her blood sugar levels were out of control, resulting in a full diabetic crisis with insulin dependency.

We shared the research of Drs. Olness and Ader with Sophia, and together we discussed the possibility of recreating a similar conditioned response, hopefully decreasing her daily dosage of the steroid, thus eliminating some of the side effects. We approached her doctor, Dr. Ola Medhat-Winn, OD, family practice specialist, with our idea and she was intrigued. Similar to Marette's situation, Sophia's use and need of prednisone had escalated to dangerous levels and something had to change. Dr. Winn was very open to our experiment, and so we began.

Using cod liver oil, Sophia began the protocol. She chose the fragrance of vanilla, and additionally added the sound of a bell. Conditioning her sense of taste, smell and sound each time she took her medication, stimulated these senses. Under the watchful eye of Dr. Winn, every other week Sophia decreased her dosage of the steroid by 5 milligrams. Slowly the drug was withdrawn, and miraculously Sophia's symptoms from lupus remained in check. The prednisone was gradually decreasing, and her blood sugars started to level and stabilize.

By conditioning with sound, taste and smell, Sophia's body was indeed learning to control the pain of lupus without the devastating side effects of the steroid. It was as if she needed the drug to tell her body how to handle the pain. Once established, the actual drug could slowly be removed, giving the body permission to heal and maintain itself, creating endorphins naturally.

Within a year, Sophia had completely eliminated her use of prednisone. Of course, the muscular aches associated with lupus remained, but to a much lesser degree, and could be controlled with mild pain medication. She continued her conditioned response of cod liver oil, vanilla musk, with the ringing of a tiny bell, and was delightfully pleased at the decrease of all the negative side effects originally created by the drug. Her sugar levels stabilized and insulin injections were replaced by an oral medication called glucotrol. Her hair, which had thinned and virtually disappeared under her arms and legs, began to grow once again.

We additionally added to Sophia's protocol the use of guided imagery. In an imagery experience, by visualizing a healthy, strong body, the process of 'remembered wellness', she slowly programmed herself back to physical strength and vitality.

Another classic conditioned response is the alpha trigger. Similar to Pavlov's dogs, we can easily create a classic conditioned response. While in a guided imagery experience, completely relaxed and calm, we often suggest that a client put their thumb and two fingers together. Either by actually making the gesture or by just imagining it in the mind, this literally becomes a cue for the brain to replicate that same feeling whenever the fingers are brought together in an awake state.

As a conditioned response, the mind will bring back that same feeling of relaxation without having to experience the imagery itself. This technique can be particularly useful in calming a client before an important meeting, stress of heavy traffic or anxiety of any kind. Often they don't have the luxury of ten or fifteen minutes to experience a calming imagery, but they can quickly put their thumb and two fingers together to create that same effect.

A client came to us years ago who was terrified of making sales presentations. This is not an uncommon problem, since studies show people are more afraid of public speaking than death. He came to see if guided imagery could help him with this fear. When he got nervous, he would even start to stutter. We did an imagery. He was told to see himself confidently speaking to a small group of people, communicating beautifully. He was not nervous. Gradually, in the experience, more and more people joined to listen to him speak, and he remained calm and assured. We told him to see himself finishing the presentation, knowing it was successful, and instructed him at that point to put his thumb and two fingers together. This is the alpha trigger, a tool he now uses before he makes a sales call or presentation.

A study was done in the 1990's by Weiland and Murphy to research the rate of healing while in different states of consciousness, such as being awake or being asleep. The study used burn victims, making it easy to literally watch the rate of growth in new skin cells in newly grafted areas. It was discovered that while these patients were awake, the average rate of cell regeneration in a 3-hour period of time was approximately 8-19 new skin cells in a 1 square millimeter of space. While the patients were asleep, this regeneration increased to 100 to 150.

Curiously, they took the experiment one step further, and while these patients were in a state of meditation, doing guided imagery, prayer, etc., the regeneration of new skin cells increased dramatically to between 400 to 450. Being relaxed in the process of guided imagery, the body starts to physically shift, the heart rate slows down, the pulse likewise slows down, the immune system is strengthened and the metabolism speeds up. The body can heal faster.

A study done in 1983 by Dr. Moore and Dr. Kaplan targeted patients with symmetrical burns. Half the group was given guided imagery to increase blood flow and healing to one side of the wound area only. Temperature of the side of focus was increased by 4 to 11 degrees, and within three days, non-partial observers were able to tell a significant difference. The target side healed 2-3 days earlier.

And, also the psychological support of imagery can reduce pain and significantly reduce anxiety during burn dressing changes. As reported by Patterson and Wilson in their research, more than 50% of their 172 burn patients experienced post-traumatic stress symptoms, such as intrusive recollections and sleep disturbance, one year after the injury. Those patients who used imagery on a daily basis found that their symptoms at one month were predictive of improvement at the one year mark.

The body can heal quicker, physically and emotionally:

- Allowing the new skin cells to regenerate quicker.
- Stimulating and increasing blood flow to the wound.
- Accelerating the immune system to fight infection.

- Reducing anxiety and pain.
- Helping to remove the psychological trauma.
- Allowing the body to sleep uninterrupted, peacefully and healthfully.

We ran across a marvelous book years ago, entitled *The Diary of a Napoleonic Foot Soldier,* written by Jakob Walter. It was a unique account of the battle from inside the ranks of Bonaparte's Grand Army. Among hundreds of ill-fed and ill-clothed young soldiers, Jakob was only 15 years old, returned home, only to be quarantined because of rampant plague.

The doctors, unable to supply the necessary medications became frustrated. One physician, Walter writes, would go from bed to bed and write down the name of the herb or tonic necessary, handing slips of paper to the soldiers. He would tell them that he didn't have the actual medicine, but instructed them to eat the words, eat the bits of paper. One by one, all the soldiers who ate the words recovered, leaving behind the rest of his platoon to die.

In the telling of this story, we are not suggesting that we throw away all our drugs and merely eat all our doctor's barely legible prescription slips. However, our faith in the efficacy of that drug can have a direct relationship to its effectiveness. If we have a strong belief in a particular medication, we increase our probability that it will work. Conversely, if we dwell on the side effects, we increase our chances of developing these conditions. Often referred to as a nocebo effect, the body quickly digests this negative information and faithfully responds, often a self-fulfilling prophecy. Just listen to all the possible negative side effects for all those drug ads on television.

Most recently there was a study done by Dr. Ted Kaptchuk, Associate Professor of Medicine at Harvard Medical. In his report, he stated that over half the internists surveyed said they believed in the placebo effect and often intentionally gave their patients ineffective medication in the hopes it would have a positive result. Kaptchuk wondered if the deception was even necessary. So, his study included 80 people suffering from irritable bowel syndrome.

Half the patients were given a bottle with the word 'placebo' printed on it, told they were merely sugar pills, and were instructed to take two pills daily. At the end of the three-week trial, 59% of the patients taking the placebo reported their symptoms had been adequately relieved, far outstripping the 35% in the no-treatment group.

A simple search on the internet will bring thousands of articles and research on the power of imagery. Belleruth Naparstek's groundbreaking work has pioneered the acceptance of guided imagery in hospitals nationwide with pre- and post-surgery, controlling side effects from chemotherapy, pain relief and even working with post-traumatic stress disorder.

SUGGESTED CHAPTER STUDY

- Suggested reading would include the marvelous books and research of Dr. Candace Pert, *Molecules of Emotions, Healing Words* by Larry Dossey, MD, *Timeless Healing* by Herbert Benson, MD and *Staying Well with Guided Imagery* by Belleruth Naparstek.

- Reinforce your belief in the power of imagery with your clients. In sharing some of these healing anecdotes and research studies, you become the placebo to their healing. In quoting Dr. Pert, *Nothing is too wonderful to be true.*

CHAPTER TWO

WHAT IS GUIDED IMAGERY

The universal language of the mind is pictures. These pictures provide a connecting link between the conscious and unconscious mind. As an individual goes into a relaxed state, they begin to see pictures; tapping into the true wisdom of this incredible mechanism we call our body.

Through these images, we can discover what is necessary to heal. The body knows exactly what it needs to gain and regain good health, if we will just listen. Aristotle was right when he said, *Medicine is just a distraction for the mind, so the body can heal itself.* Psychologist, Dr. Jeanne Achterberg, often describes this process of imagery as being, *The midwife that births feelings from the unconscious to the conscious mind,* affording healing both physically and emotionally.

Freud claimed that the unconscious mind occupied ninety percent and the conscious mind only ten percent of our brain function, and felt that all our true motives and causes for behavior were buried beneath our conscious awareness. The implication is that all of us function from unconscious motivation.

Psychologist, Gordon Allport, elaborated that the unhealthier you are, the more you function from the unconscious. The healthier you are, the more you function from conscious awareness. This concept is aligned with our philosophy of IntraPersonal Imagery. We use guided imagery to resolve deeply buried issues of the past and change the unconscious belief systems to conform with those of our conscious choices as adults. Then the unconscious mind becomes more in harmony with the adult beliefs of today. There is little or no conflict between the two.

In Allport's words, *We are primarily functioning from conscious awareness – today's beliefs and values – rather than being compelled by the issues of the past.* Once resolved and changed, these issues are no longer buried in the past and controlling our perceptions and behavior.

Freud added, *Dreams are the royal road to the unconscious.* Dreams and their interpretations have been a vital aspect of understanding ourselves since the beginning of time. The difficulty with dreams, however, is that they must be remembered in order to be interpreted and the predictability of an epiphany or revelation occurring in sleep cannot be guaranteed.

Guided Imagery, on the other hand, can be a dependable transportation down Freud's royal road. Imagery is a dream in the waking state. The person is equally relaxed as in the dream state, but the conscious mind is more tuned in to listen. The dream or imagery can be created at will with no restrictions. This act of creation gives instant access to whatever subject we wish to address, rather than waiting for the dream to decide.

Carl Jung called his version of guided imagery *Active Imagination* and discovered that the unconscious mind was in a sense constantly dreaming. Since the individual's attention is focused on the external, they are unaware of the mythic story that is continually developing unless they stop to focus on it. Jung remarked, *When you concentrate on a mental picture it begins to stir, the image becomes enriched by details. It moves and develops, and so when we concentrate on inner pictures and we are careful not to interrupt the natural flow of events, our unconscious will produce a series of images that makes a complete story.*

Jung's explanation remains one of the simplest and clearest definitions of what guided imagery is and does. He further commented that, *This active imagination process was superior to dreams in defeating the unconscious for a quickening of maturation in analysis.* In other words, imagery is superior to dreams in overcoming or defeating the unconscious mind's resistance to allowing buried truth to come to conscious awareness. Bringing this truth to the surface, where it can be acknowledged and properly dealt with, speeds up the therapeutic growth in analysis.

Hanscarl Leuner MD, a German analyst, called his basic level of imagery, *A superior short term therapy that closes the gap between symptom-centered procedures and the great psychoanalytic cure.* Symptom-centered procedures refer to types of therapy that focus on immediate results by solving the problem or changing the acting-out behavior of the client, without regard for the original cause. The great psychoanalytic cure, as Leuner refers to, is the Freudian approach of finding and curing the original source of the symptom, which could take years.

What is this simple but mysterious and powerful procedure called guided imagery? It is a relaxation process that helps a person to shut off the outside world of rational logic, to by-pass that censor we call the brain, enabling us to see, experience, and learn from our intuitive, feeling and unconscious nature.

Many people are afraid of feelings, fearing they are untrustworthy, essentially bad or destructive, believing that their emotions will lead them astray into their animal nature. All of us, however, are complex creatures of intellect and emotion, feelings and doings. Feelings are the barometer of the soul. They tell the intellect what the issues are. The job of the intellect is to interpret, understand, and decide appropriate reactions. To function effectively as human beings we need all aspects of self in harmony, balance and open communication.

When a therapist works with guided imagery, he or she induces a state of relaxation and then suggests that the client visualize a scene. The therapist guides the client through some experience that results in an insight. Consider this example of a guided imagery session:

See your mother as an animal.
If she were an animal what would she be?

I see a rather large cow, contently chewing her cud in a green pasture. There are two little calves nearby, occasionally coming over for milk.

What is your overall impression?
Passive and quiet. She seems content.

What do you like best and least?
Best is the peacefulness and lack of stress. Least is that the cow is lazy, unmotivated, fat and indolent, a dirty farm animal with no real purpose.

Become the cow. What do you feel?
Contented but bored. I feel judged by my daughter. My life doesn't have any real purpose.

The therapist could have asked the client to describe her mother and how she felt about her. But, the client's intellect may have struggled with guilt or anger, or perhaps even been more superficial in the description. But, by seeing mother as an animal, the client is able to describe the animal as seen in the moment rather than the actual mother. The unconscious mind gives us subtle information we may otherwise avoid. And there is less guilt. This is what they saw, not what they decided to see, or felt would be the correct thing to see.

The value of guided imagery is that this process can diagnose a problem, provide options for change, and even promote healing and personal empowerment. However, the primary purpose is to allow the body to relax, healing the physical and emotional aspects of self. Any new insights gained during an imagery experience are an added bonus to personal growth.

The next step in the process of imagery is to allow unresolved anger, conflict, trauma and fear, which may be deeply buried in the unconscious, to emerge into the light of conscious awareness. Once seen clearly, these issues can easily be understood and related to more appropriately.

One of our guided imagery graduates wrote, *Why did guided imagery have such benefit after years of laying on the couch and experiencing talk therapy? I couldn't bring myself to talk about the trauma. I couldn't give it a voice. I would experience vivid symbolic dreams. Then I would feel pain in my jaw. I had other symbolic dreams, but I couldn't get to the cause. The dreams were driving me insane and I went into a serious depression. Then I did guided imagery and the answers became available to me by way of my subconscious mind. While I was fearful, I got to the trauma in a much less threatening form of therapy. Because of the relaxation, the music, and giving permission to the subconscious to see what perhaps we can't talk about in an awake state, the word that comes to mind is 'safe'.*

This kind of imagery has been successfully used in healing cancer and other illnesses, for pain control, for relieving the emotional trauma of war, incest or abuse, for overcoming phobias, or for habit control such as addictions, as well as understanding self better. This technique is a powerful, fun, amazing form of personal insight that can take us from a place of personal healing to ultimate empowerment and fulfillment.

Whether through guided imagery or dreams, the unconscious is presenting us with stories filled with images and symbols. Understanding their meaning can enhance their impact and the importance of the information.

UNIVERSAL SYMBOLS

A universal symbol is one that usually means the same to all people regardless of race, culture, time, or place. Our students often ask what determines a universal symbol. From the beginning of time, scholars have studied dreams and the mythology of every culture. All religions, myths, dreams, fairy tales, even movies of today tell the same stories with the same symbolism and meaning.

Jung referred to these symbols or archetypes as embedded information in our psyches that mean the same for everyone. He coined the expression 'morphic resonance', and theorized that, *An event or act can lead to similar events or acts in the future, or an idea or belief conceived in one mind can then arise in another.* There is more and more evidence that we may even carry these archetypal symbols and beliefs in our DNA from generation to generation.

For example, the earth is a prominently universal symbol. It is called 'mother earth' because it plays out the role of universal mother. The seed is impregnated and planted in the ground and grows for a period of time and then it is born. Once born it is fed and nourished by the earth, an exact description of the mother role.

PARTICULAR OR PERSONAL SYMBOLS

The second type of symbol is a particular or personal symbol and refers to what it means to the individual. For example, George has a dream that he is walking a narrow mountain path and the earth gives way beneath his feet. He slips and falls twenty feet and breaks his ankle. The universal interpretation might suggest that he is walking a narrow path, on the edge, so to speak, with his mother. Since the universal symbol of ankle tends to represent instability in a present situation, perhaps his mother has disappointed him or let him down in some way, hence the breaking of his ankle.

George says he has an excellent relationship with a very supportive mother, and that interpretation doesn't fit. The therapist might ask George, "What's going on in your life right now?" And George's reply might be that a friend of his invited him to go hiking next week and he's afraid he won't be able to keep up or possibly he will injure himself. Now the dream is more personal and makes sense.

Someone else might share that they had a dream of being attacked by a ten-foot, black widow spider. The dream is loaded with universal symbols. Black is a symbol of evil or bad. In the old cowboy movies, the guys in the black hats and clothes were the outlaws and the ones in white were the good guys. The black widow spider is a female who is poisonous and kills. Being ten-foot tall is a symbol of exaggeration. The dreamer is blowing his fear way out of proportion to reality.

On the other hand, women love this story. They consistently complain that men use them for sex and then cast them aside. Here the female, the spider, gets even. She uses her mate to fertilize her many eggs and when she no longer needs him, for he is only a sperm donor, she poisons and kills him and then eats him. In interpreting the dream the therapist might ask, "Who is the woman who is overwhelmingly scaring you to death?" She could be a mother, wife, daughter, sister, boss or even an event such as a final exam.

Suppose however, there are no women in the dreamer's life. The interpretation doesn't fit. A further question to ask might be, "Is that why there are no women in your life, you see them as black widow spiders?" But, after further probing, convinced that the universal symbols or interpretations don't resonate, a further question could be, "What was going on at the time of the dream?"

With some confusion, the client might answer, "I'm working 12-14 hours a day and feel totally overwhelmed by responsibility. I don't feel I can possibly catch up or do it right." In this case, the job itself is symbolized by the black widow spider, overwhelmingly destructive and killing him.

The particular interpretation could also be a literal one. The client has a very real fear or phobia of spiders. But even if the literal meaning is true, the deeper symbolic interpretation underlying the obvious could be that this person feels like a victim in life. No matter how many spiders he kills or problems he solves, he will inevitably wind up a victim or loser. Thus, a symbol can represent a person, a particular situation or even a belief system.

OBJECTIVE INTERPRETATION

The objective interpretation is how we see our outside world. That means every symbol in a dream or imagery represents someone or something in the world. Using the black widow spider as an example, the spider objectively represents someone or something outside: a mother, a wife, a daughter, a job. If there were six different symbols in a dream, all of them could represent someone or something specific.

THE SUBJECTIVE INTERPRETATION

The subjective interpretation means how we perceive our inside world. All the symbols in a dream or imagery represent a part within the self. Therefore, the black widow spider is the poisonous, feminine, evil side of us. Which is better, the objective or subjective approach to interpreting symbols? The exciting answer is that it doesn't matter. They are highly correlated and either will accomplish the same goal.

That correlation is the basis of the book we wrote, *The Conflict Between Us is the Conflict Within Me.* If you are the black widow spider, aggressive and dominant, who will you marry? The incompatible opposite, which would be a passive, obedient, submissive victim.

INCOMPATIBLE OPPOSITES

Aggressor _____ Victim
^

If you go to therapy to save your marriage and you become less aggressive and dominant and your partner becomes more assertive and self sufficient, you have both moved to the middle and saved the marriage.

More Gentle _____ More Assertive
^

In the imagery process, the couple has healed the black widow spider within. Both have used the external problem to heal the inner conflict. For point of reference, either one could be so fearful of the spider within, that it is denied and disowned. As a result, the individual becomes nice, generous, and passive. This nice person would then marry the spider and the process is reversed.

On the other hand, the woman could go to therapy alone, because her partner wouldn't or because she prefers to work on herself. She learns to deal with her own 'spider meanness' and works towards center by making peace with unresolved anger, which heals the personal 'spider' within.

How does that affect the relationship? As she moves towards center, she begins acting differently towards her partner. If her husband responds appropriately and likes the change, he in turn moves to center and the relationship is improved, finding a healing. One spouse can go to therapy and save a marriage without the other spouse.

If, however, your mate is repelled by the changes and your consequential move toward center, they will move further away, trying to maintain the original balance or incompatibility. In that case, one of you at some point will leave because you no longer compliment each other's extremes. The balance, however precarious, is destroyed.

There has to be a 'dance of balance' or a 'dance of distance' and polarity. There really is no other choice. When there are unresolved issues within us, the tendency is to externalize them within a relationship. All outer conflicts are balanced by inner ones. Cure one and the other heals, too.

IMAGERY AND THE MIND-BODY CONNECTION

Just as there is a connection between the interior battle of dominance and passivity within all of us that externalizes in our man/woman relationships, there is also a similar turf war between the scientific and therapeutic worlds about what effects the mind and body really have over each other. For over a century, therapists have witnessed clinical, anecdotal evidence that relaxation procedures, such as guided imagery and hypnosis, promote both physical and emotional healing, but there was no way to measure this scientifically.

Years ago, biofeedback gave evidence that we can control the autonomic nervous system and today, with modern technology, scientists can now track activity in the brain or use blood samples to prove that behavior, thoughts, and feelings can bring about instant changes in the physical body.

While the conflict between heredity and environment raged on for years as to which had the most influence, there is more and more evidence that heredity is not necessarily locked in at birth, and that it is constantly interacting with the environment to bring out a new and different self every day of our lives. In the words of best selling author, Caroline Myss, *Our biography becomes our biology.* The very way we think, feel, act and believe is effecting and changing our physical bodies.

People have often interpreted psychosomatic behavior as an imaginary illness created in our head. 'Psycho' refers to the mind and 'somatic' to the body. The true meaning is that the mind can make the body ill or well, and the body can do the same to the mind. All physical and emotional issues are connected. The miracle of guided imagery is its ability to approach all problems from either the physical or the emotional side and yet heal both, often simultaneously.

HOW DOES THE BODY GET SICK?

Most of us would like to credit outside influences, the flu, infections, or disease that are spread from the environment, as the cause of our illness, but even in an epidemic, not everyone gets sick. We all carry germs and disease in our bodies daily and we don't get ill. The immune system is designed to kill these germs to keep us well. So why do we sometimes become sick?

In simple terms, we don't listen to ourselves and often violate or contradict our basic belief systems. The body, therefore, goes out of balance and the immune system becomes less efficient. Anything unresolved, such as anger, stress, or pain, creates inner conflict.

The various sub-personalities within us start fighting among themselves to solve the problem. The body fights to compensate and keep a sense of order. For instance, your right shoulder tenses up and throws the left hip out of alignment, causing sciatic pain. This is a defensive attempt of the body to balance itself or to tell you that something is wrong.

FIVE STEPS TO HEALING THE BODY THROUGH INTRAPERSONAL IMAGERY

Over the years, we have found a rather simple, five step approach for using imagery as a healing tool. Guided imagery is used by many people in myriad fashion, as can be said of any medical or therapeutic technique. There is no one right way to do anything.

For simplicity and clarity, the illustrations of imagery that follow will address the physical side of healing, but the physical is interchangeable with the emotional. You could be directed to find an infection or tumor in your body or you could also be directed to locate where the energetic influence of your mother resides in your body. The healing process would basically be the same.

RELAX THE BODY

The first step in imagery is to induce a relaxed state of being. Just by closing our eyes, taking a deep breath, our body begins to calm down. Our heart rate slows down, likewise the pulse, and the immune system is actually stimulated.

More and more we are becoming aware of the importance of the immune system as the wellspring of our good health, both physically and emotionally; a miraculous mechanism of defense and repair of our organs. The immune system is directly influenced by the cells in our brain. Psychoneuroimmunology, the study of the interaction between the brain and the immune system, suggests that we can affect our body's health through these guided imagery techniques. Seeing our body become healthy through our mind's eye is the key and first step towards healing.

Cleveland researchers compared a group of people who received standard care with those who, for three days before surgery, and six days after, listened to audio cassettes, combining vocal instruction and soothing music. *The guided imagery group described their pain as half as severe, used one third less medication, and left the hospital sooner.*

Dr. Herbert Benson recommends the imagery experience of bathing the body with a healing solution. In this relaxation, the brain will actually start to release endorphins, serotonins and various chemicals in the body to relieve pain, enhance and speed the healing process. Through this visualization process we can literally get out of our own way, allowing the body to naturally mend, promote good health and well being. For the body knows how to be healthy.

Have you ever had a charley-horse? That's the cramp in the leg muscle that wakes one up in the morning. Most of us tense up to fight the pain, and the pain gets worse, tension against tension. It's impossible to relax the cramp, so relax 'into' the pain. Relax the rest of the body and the pain can spread out and be released more easily. Prepared childbirth and the use of effleurage is the same principle. The contraction is needed to deliver the baby, so by relaxing the rest of the body, the pain becomes more bearable.

VISUALIZE THE PAIN

The next step is to look at any painful spot in the body and describe it, such as tight muscles, red inflammation, a cut or tear, an actual tumor or just a blackened area. Some individuals will not see body afflictions, but will see symbols of the pain instead, such as fire, demons, an arrow or knife, an iron band squeezing the head, or a knotted, tight rope.

The unconscious has a great sense of humor and often uses puns to make a point. If a person sees bugs crawling all over a part of the body, the question might simply be, "What's bugging you?" If a stabbing pain in the rib cage is symbolized as a sharp knife stuck deep between the ribs, you might ask, "Who or what is stabbing you or inflicting pain in your life?" If a client sees a monkey clinging powerfully to his back, the question might be, "Who is the monkey on your back?"

TALK TO THE PAIN

Once we have an image of this physical and/or emotional pain, the next step is to talk to it. Amazingly, the symbol will usually be very happy to respond. There is no wrong way to do guided imagery. We may see, sense, hear or just know, but answers will come.

Here are sample questions to identify what the pain is connected to, and what can be done to relieve it:

- What is the original cause of this pain?
- What is the most important thing the pain wants me to know about it?
- What do you want from me that you're not getting?
- How would my life be different if I gave it to you?
- What do I need to do to allow this pain to heal?

It is very important to see all pain as a messenger of truth. The pain is either trying to tell us something or trying to hide something from us. How are we to distinguish between the two choices? The following examples may help.

One client had a twenty year history of migraine headaches that were so severe she considered suicide. This woman was in a very abusive marriage but carried a religious belief that divorce was a sin and, therefore, not an option for her. In imagery, the headache told her the only solution for her was to get a divorce. The day she left her husband, the headaches went away and never returned. Before she learned the truth, we could say the headaches were trying to distract her from a bad marriage and provide distance from an abusive husband so she could stay.

Another woman suffered from chronic backache throughout years in a troubled marriage to an alcoholic. When he died, the backaches spontaneously went away. The body may become ill as a way of creating a dependency to justify staying in the marriage. It is extremely important to get as much information as possible from the pain before any action is taken.

REMOVE THE PAIN

Many people are not capable or ready to remove pain, even if they want to. The pain often becomes a part of their identity. "If I'm not a victim of this pain, who am I?" In the words of the famous Carly Simon song, *Suffering is the only way that makes me feel alive.* Or, the pain might be protecting them from having to take responsibility for themselves before they are ready.

There are several steps involved with removing pain:

- Without hurting yourself or the symbol, take it in your hands and gently remove the symbol from your body.
- While holding the pain, send it love. In its own distorted way, this pain is trying to protect you from what it perceives as a greater threat or pain. What happens to the pain when you send it love? Does it change in some manner?

- You are now being offered a magic solution. This solution is made up of chemicals from your own body that knows better than you or a doctor or a therapist exactly what is needed to heal this pain. Spray or administer this magic solution liberally. What happens to the symbol or pain when you do this?
- Put the pain or symbol on a shelf. Even if you are not ready to let go of this issue, put it on the shelf for a short time. Tell the pain that it needs a rest from working so hard and your body does, too. You can always go back and pick it up again later.
- Fill the space in the body where the pain was removed with the magic or healing solution. What happens to the spot when you do that?

A word about the magic solution. Some people don't like to use the word 'magic' in connection with the healing process, with possible connotations such as fraud, not real, too mystical, etc. If you like, call it a healing solution. We often use the two together, a magic, healing solution. We use the word magic because it truly is out of our conscious control – the body's own placebo – and therefore feels magical and exciting. This is healing on the unconscious level, where real and permanent change can take place.

HEALING AND TRANSFORMATION

By removing the pain or symbol, the healing process has already begun. Sending love and the magic solution continues the healing process to a deeper level. Remember, we are not removing a part of ourselves. Infection, cancer, or emotional pains are not a part of us. We can now deal with these issues, physical or emotional, including parents, marriages, and careers, from outside the body. When touched by love and the magic solution, the symbol itself will often turn from something ugly and menacing to something smaller, more colorful and pleasant. If you see red infection, it may turn to skin tone, demons could change to small children, and fires are diminished or go out.

The body has been given permission to heal itself. Negative energy can be transformed to positive energy as perceptions change and fears subside. Sometimes, the client or the therapist will create a ritual of healing to complete the process, such as floating in a pool filled with the magic solution to cleanse and purify the entire body.

This simple, five step process, can be modified to work with any emotional or physical pain or issue in our life. The imagery process just described may sound mysterious or even preposterous to someone who has never experienced it, but thousands of people have found that this method provides the relaxed, safe, and loving environment which enables healing, restoration, and empowerment for new perceptions, choices, and opportunities.

Research is continually validating that the body knows how to heal. We can give permission to our incredible anatomy to heal naturally. Through this process of imagery, we can identify and remove these blocks from our body, whether physical or emotional, and return to health and well being. Imagery is equally effective for relationship dysfunction as well as for physical healing. Earlier we gave an example of seeing your mother as an animal. Let's use that same format for a marital relationship.

QUICK IMAGERY
PARTNER OR SPOUSE AS AN ANIMAL

Read each sentence and then stop and allow your mind to wander and imagine. Let anything come that wants to come.

See your partner or spouse as an animal.

If they were an animal, what would it be? Go with the first animal that appears and try not to edit.

Describe the animal as to type, size, color and attitude.

What is the setting in which you find this animal?

What is your overall impression of this animal?

What do you like best about this animal? What do you like least?

How does the animal respond to you?

What happens when you approach it?

Now, become the animal. See if you can actually be the animal and feel what it is feeling. What do you feel as the animal?

As the animal, look back at the person in front of you. How do you feel about this person?

As the animal, make a statement to the person.

Become yourself again.

How do you feel about what the animal said to you?

You can change the animal in any way you choose or leave it the way it is.

You can put the animal anywhere you choose or leave it where you found it.

Now, slowly and deliberately, let yourself come back to this room.

Once the imagery has been completed, take some time to write down what you actually saw and experienced. Then come back to this section. Use the script to help you remember the events you experienced. What did you learn about your spouse by seeing them as an animal? The type of animal can be very revealing: a grizzly bear or a teddy bear, a cunning fox or slimy snake, overwhelmingly large or small and inadequate. What was the general attitude of this animal? Was it friendly, trusting, angry, loving, dominant or submissive? What was your first overall impression? Remember, there is no Judgment here. Whatever you saw and felt is ok, it's your experience.

What you liked best and least can add to the experience. This can supply important clues to hidden or obscure feelings. One husband described his wife in glowing terms as a beautiful, fluffy Siamese cat, warm and loving, but finished by saying he was always aware that hidden in those soft, gentle paws were claws of steel that could tear him to shreds. His wife saw him as a knight in shining armor on his horse, always ready to defend her, but she never lost sight of the fact he could easily use that sword on her.

Becoming the animal is an important step toward empathy. Experiencing the world of someone else through their eyes can be quite revealing. One woman saw her husband as an angry, wild, hostile lion. When she became the lion, she was shocked to feel frightened and helpless, terrified of being wrong or inadequate. What was your experience? What did you learn about your spouse, yourself, and your relationship?

Is guided imagery for everyone? Over the years, we have found just a handful of people who were not able to relax enough to do imagery for a variety of reasons: fear of what information might come up, exposure to self or others, fear that they couldn't do it, or fear of being hypnotized and under someone else's control.

Since guided imagery is very similar to hypnosis, this issue sometimes comes up. The difference between the two is mostly the manner in which the therapist or facilitator was trained. Much of hypnosis training concerns behavior modification for breaking addictive habits or phobias, or for giving positive affirmations. The way that any therapist would use either imagery or hypnosis would be greatly influenced by their theoretic orientation and background.

As for control, people who have seen stage hypnotists have a difficult time believing that the person maintains choice during the event. In our approach, we explain that there is no need for control or desire to change someone or something. The emphasis of our imagery is to reveal information for better understanding, clarity and choice. It's the client's journey, not the therapist's.

SUGGESTED CHAPTER STUDY

- Understand the difference between universal and particular symbols. How a client interprets any symbol trumps the universal meaning, however a good grasp of universal meanings can enhance the discussion after the imagery. We've provided a directory of some of the more common symbols, located in the Appendix. Also, a good dream dictionary can enhance your knowledge of what many symbols would tend to represent.

- 'The Five Steps to Healing' is the basic philosophy of IntraPersonal imagery. We've given you the examples of seeing a physical pain, seeing a parent, seeing a spouse or partner. Can you think of other issues your clients could bring that could be incorporated into this process?

CHAPTER THREE

FIRST THINGS FIRST –
THE INDUCTION

The essential prerequisite for any form of guided imagery to work effectively is a complete state of deep relaxation, leading the client to an altered state of consciousness, which in essence is lowering their brain-waves. There are four primary brain-wave patterns: Beta, Alpha, Theta and Delta rhythms, all of which are contained within a total energy spectrum of about 0 to 30 cycles per second or Hz.

BETA

Beta waves, 13 – 30 Hz, are most typically associated with normal waking states in which we are focused on external stimulus. Beta is our basic survival orientation, and is most present when we are computing, arranging, organizing, sorting out and making sense of our external world. Beta is increased in moments of anxiety, enabling us to manage situations and solve immediate problems. In today's world of the internet, instant messages, and the speed of information bombarding us, scientists are discovering an increased brain-wave pattern. The Gamma waves, functioning at around 40 Hz, increase stress, but provide even greater multi-tasking abilities.

ALPHA

Alpha waves, 7 – 13 Hz, indicate an alert state with a quiet mind. In this state, attention may be focused outward for problem-solving, or inward to achieve an alert meditative state. Alpha may be dominant in states of focused concentration or in the attainment of a still inner center. Increased Alpha is often present in the brain-wave patterns of people who practice meditation, yoga and tai chi, for example, and also essential for any imagery experience.

THETA

Theta waves, 3 – 7 Hz, reflect a mind state that is associated with deep meditation and daydreaming. Theta waves are dominant during rapid eye movement, REM sleep, where most dreams take place. Theta is often associated with creativity and artistic endeavors.

DELTA

Delta waves, 0.1 – 3 Hz, are associated with the deepest levels of physical relaxation. The slowest of the brain-wave frequencies, Delta is the rhythm of dreamless sleep. Their presence is usually associated with physical rejuvenation and healing. That would explain why when we are sick, we need to sleep.

Through the process of doing a guided imagery, lowering the brain-waves to Alpha is essential. The Alpha state is usually associated with feelings of detachment and yet is accompanied by alertness, like having a dream in an awake state. This serene feeling state, often referred to as an 'alpha high', is accompanied by a lack of anxiety and judgment. Therefore, the goal of any imagery is the process of establishing and maintaining this 7 to 13 Hz, with even periods of the client lowering to Theta.

This Alpha state can be reached most successfully by talking the client into relaxation. This is called an induction. Since excessive amounts of speaking or verbal content in an induction can actually keep a client in the conscious mode and can reduce or even inhibit or block the creation of beneficial images, keep the induction simple. Also, research is showing that it takes the average brain about 4 to 5 minutes to slow down to Alpha. The induction, therefore, should be about 5 minutes to make sure the client has reached this point of relaxation.

YOUR VOICE

The induction process is as much for your benefit as the therapist, as it is for the client. Be aware of your cadence slowing down and the pitch of your voice softening. The law of entrainment will afford the client to slow down as you slow down and relax.

Resonant entrainment is a well understood principal within the physical sciences. In 1665, Dutch scientist Christian Huygens discovered that two pendulum clocks mounted side-by-side on the same wall would gradually begin to swing at the same rate. He found that this held true consistently as if they wanted to assume the same rhythm. From his investigations came the theory and understanding of what is today termed 'entrainment'. In the case of the two pendulums, one is said to entrain the other to its frequency.

Similarly, if a tuning fork designed to produce a frequency of 440 Hz, for example, is struck, a second tuning fork in its vicinity, similarly designed to vibrate at 440 Hz, will begin to vibrate. This sympathetic vibration is also an example of entrainment. The first tuning fork is said to have entrained the second.

So strong is the natural tendency towards entrainment that in one interesting experiment, a researcher set up a wave of a desired frequency in a water bed. When a research subject rested on the bed, the resulting tactile signals were effective in entraining the subject's brain-waves to the selected frequency.

This same principal of entrainment can be applied to influence human brain-wave patterns. Studies using EEG equipment to measure brain-waves show a clear correlation between brain-wave response and external pulses experienced by the subject. Initially, research in this area used pulsing light flashes, but later this effect was found to work with a variety of different pulse phenomena, including sound pulses and even electromagnetic pulses. If pulses at a consistent frequency are introduced into the brain by visual, audio or electrical means, the brain has a natural tendency to follow, or lock into their frequency. This is called 'frequency following response'. So, as the therapist during the induction, as you start to slow down and lower your own brain-wave frequency to this Alpha place, the client will engage in the frequency following response.

YOUR LANGUAGE

Using the theory of Neurolinguistics, try to feed back to the client the words that they use, that they are comfortable with. Are they visual thinkers? Are they kinesthetic? Are they auditory? One of the most powerful aspects in the study of Neurolinguistic Programming, commonly referred to as NLP, is systems analysis. Science has proven that people process differently, each of us thinks in a different language. These languages are directly related to the five senses. We take in information through our sight, smell, taste, touch and sound, and we literally process or think in terms of these senses.

Systems analysis claims that through this sensory input, we all tend to favor one sense as the primary framework in which we think and communicate and even experience imagery. The person who is highly visual, always sees the big picture, is someone who processes information through sight. The person who is more directed by feelings is thinking through their sense of touch and is kinesthetic. Many people are driven by sounds, communicating in terms such as, "I hear what you're saying," and are auditory.

Less common, there are those who process information through their sense of taste. Memories are tied strongly to foods and the various stimulations to the tongue, and are referred to as gustatory. Far less frequent, there are people who think using the sense of smell, highly motivated by aromas, referred to as olfactory. They would commonly use expressions such as, "I smell something fishy." The smell of freshly baked bread could trigger a childhood experience very quickly. Wake up and smell the coffee.

To help a client through an imagery, speaking in words and terms that relate to their sense of choice will definitely enhance their experience. Be sensitive to how your client communicates and the words they use to assess whether they are visual, kinesthetic, auditory, gustatory or olfactory. If you determine that they are visual, speak back to them and incorporate your imagery dialogue to include how things look, what they see, etc. If your client is kinesthetic, ask questions such as, "How do you feel about that?" The gustatory person will enjoy your statement of, "Lick your lips and taste the salt water."

Rather than getting too caught up in the process of NLP, however, we strongly recommend that in the induction, you stimulate all the senses. For example, you might add these questions and ask the following questions:

Look around, what do you see?
What do you feel?
Listen, what are the sounds?
What are the aromas that you smell?
Lick your lips, what are the tastes that you experience?

You've covered all the bases. The client will surely resonate to one or more of these senses. And further, since we all process and think differently, we all experience imagery differently. Some will actually see the experience as if they are watching a movie, others will just sense it. However the imagery is perceived, the information is being received. Remember, there's no right way or wrong way to do it.

MUSIC

In the background, provide soft music that is simple. Complicated melodies may distract the client. Avoid music that has vocal or shifts in rhythm. Try to find a selection that is continuous for at least 30 minutes. Sometimes the changing of a track may be distracting. Again, the law of entrainment applies, and the client will slow down to the tempo of the music. According to Belleruth Naparstek, the efficacy of the imagery experience is increased considerably when music is used.

The introduction of music is extremely helpful in enhancing this relaxed state. Choose music that is soothing and low, and has a simple gentle rhythm. Extensive research is being conducted by such pioneers as Don Campbell at the Denver Institute of Sound, and the actual vibrations and frequencies of sound can bring us peace, as well as discord. The use of simple nature sounds can be extremely beneficial.

The more complicated the music, the more difficult it becomes to relax. The music you choose should have no lyrics. Also, recognizable melodies should be avoided, since in many cases, the client will start to remember the song and begin to associate with memories wrapped around that particular piece of music.

Find a piece of music that you can get comfortable with, and you enjoy. Remember, the job of the induction is to relax the therapist, as well as the client. Once the client is in the Alpha state, they are basically unaware of the music. You may even want to turn the volume down once the induction is complete.

We use the music of Mark Provost, Solara Recording and Production, exclusively for all our guided imageries. Mark is our audio engineer who records and produces all our imagery CDs, and is a graduate of our guided imagery certification program. He is very sensitive to the importance of music during an imagery experience and has created some marvelous music with each piece being at least thirty minutes in length, making it seamless for any imagery adventure. You can listen to samples of Mark's music at www.musicforguidedimagery.com.

PHYSICAL CUES

As you do the induction, watch your client. You will get physical cues that they are beginning to relax. Shoulders may drop, legs uncross, hands open up and breathing slows down. Even with their eyes closed, you can see the eyes moving back and forth; that rapid eye movement associated with lowering brain-waves.

We believe the induction is the most critical part of the total experience. If the induction is ineffective and the client never reaches that relaxed Alpha state, the experience will become mute. So, as the therapist, create and embrace one or two inductions that are in your own words that you can deliver in a relaxed, comfortable and intimate tone. Have fun creating this beginning journey to the world of possibilities called guided imagery.

To summarize, first and foremost, the induction is the vehicle to get the client into a relaxed state and lower the brain-waves to that Alpha frequency. Create a simple experience of peace and calm, nothing complicated; just a journey to feel peaceful, safe and serene. Within the induction, this affords you, the therapist, the opportunity to relax also. Since the client will be entraining to you, your projection of peace and calm is vital.

Your beginning words in starting any induction should include phrases such as:

Just relax.
Gently close your eyes and get comfortable.
Take a deep breath
Slowly breathing in through your nose and out through your mouth.
And again.
With every breath, feel your body begin to relax.

We have found that just by the simple act of conscious breathing, the body starts to calm down. You may even take a few deep breaths yourself along with your client. As Charlotte Reznick shares in her book, *The Power of Your Child's Imagination*, deep breathing is the cornerstone of all meditative practices. In her work with children, Dr. Reznick has developed a technique called *The Balloon Breath* and states, *A deep, diaphragmatic breath fills the body like a balloon, from the bottom. It's the belly, not the chest, that rises and falls first.* Once this technique is mastered, she continues, *the child has found 'the way in' to his private world; that world of guided imagery.*

Following are a few suggestions in creating your own inductions. Make them your own, using your own words, delivered in self-assurance and confidence. In the Appendix, we have provided four induction scripts, which will provide you some ideas to get started.

THE BODY IN COLOR

Centuries ago, the Hindu culture developed a system of identifying energy within the physical body, called Chakras. In Sanskrit, the word means 'wheel' or 'turning'. This theory includes seven electro magnetic fields within the body, each location corresponding to a different color, and with an actual meaning or emotion associated with each area. Dr. Candace Pert, the renowned biochemist, honors this system as blending ancient wisdom with modern science, with each Chakra being an actual mini-brain within the body. Her work reveals that, *Each point has electrical and chemical activity that receives, processes and distributes information from and to the rest of the mind-body.*

Whether you believe in this theory or not, whether your client knows about Charkas or not, an induction of focusing on the base of the spine working upward through the body to the head, activating and moving through the anatomy, thus stimulating the various areas and their associated colors, can be a great induction. No need to even mention the word 'Chakra'.

1st Chakra	Base of Spine	
	Grounding and Safety – Red	
2nd Chakra	Sexual Organs	
	Creativity – Orange	
3rd Chakra	Solar Plexus	
	Self-Esteem and Confidence – Yellow	
4th Chakra	Heart	
	Healing and Expressing Love – Green	
5th Chakra	Throat	
	Speaking Truth, Spoken or Written – Blue	
6th Chakra	Forehead	
	Intuition and Devotion – Purple	
7th Chakra	Top of Head	
	Spirituality, Peace and Wisdom – White	

In our studies of the Chakra system, we have discovered an eighth area, the thymus, which is located right below the throat. The color associated is turquoise and carries the symbolism of knowing your truth; a powerful correlation with the blue of speaking your truth. How often we speak without truly formulating our personal authenticity, integrity and truth.

Using this type of induction, move the client up through the various areas using the associated colors as indicated above. Start from the base of the spine and work your way up to the top of the head. Progressing upwards affords the client more connection to their spiritual or psychic side. Reversing the Chakras and beginning at the crown and working your way down affords the client more access to their body and physical healing. Ending with the first Charka of security and grounding to earth, this induction is great to end the day and prepare someone for a restful sleep.

Using the Chakras, you could progress them to any one of the locations, depending on what type of issue you are addressing. If the client is working on finding their truth or speaking their truth, you may want to take them to blue, the throat Chakra, and just stay there and begin the experience. Likewise, if the client is working on physical healing, you may want to take them to the green in the heart Chakra, or yellow in the Solar Plexus, if there are issues of self-esteem and confidence.

HEAD DOWN – WHITE LIGHT

Start at the top of the head and gradually bring the light down the whole body. Pay attention to all the body parts as you work your way down. This is the easiest way to relax someone, since you are beginning the relaxation process with the smallest muscles in the body, the face and around the eyes, then working down to the largest muscles, the legs.

Before suggesting that the light is warm or cool, check with your client. What would be most comfortable for them? During one of our sessions with a client, we did an induction using a beautiful, warming light cascading down the body, relaxing every part in warmth. It was clearly evident that this induction was not working. We gently invited her, without going any further into the imagery, to come back to this room and open her eyes. Her eyes popped open immediately and she said, "My menopause and these hot flashes are terrible. I'm dying here with this warm light!"

RHYTHM AND ENTRAINMENT – OCEAN

There is a frequency and vibration to everything in nature. Curiously the frequency of the ocean is about 12.478 Hz, which is within the Alpha cycle. The body definitely entrains to this frequency. It seems like most people truly find relaxation and peace at the beach, entraining to that lower vibration.

Start the induction by inviting a client to be on a beach, perhaps saying, "Look around, feel a gentle breeze and an ocean mist on your face. Wiggle your toes in the damp sand. See the sea gulls flying around." Perhaps even have them walk up to the shore line and feel the cool water of each wave caressing their feet, and as the wave recedes, feel the sand shift under their feet. Check with your client first, however, to make sure they are comfortable with the ocean. If they have a fear of water or have had trauma in their past that involved water or the ocean, understandably, this would not be a good choice for a relaxing induction to begin an imagery experience.

PLACE OF PEACE

In doing a guided imagery with a group where everyone is having a silent experience, the induction could include suggestions such as, "Find a place in your imagination where you feel safe and relaxed. It can be a real place where you find comfort and calm, or a place you've heard or read about, or perhaps it's an imaginary place. Wherever that is, just be there." Experience all five senses; see, hear, smell, taste and feel.

Look around, where are you?
What do you see?
What are the sounds in your place of peace?
What's the temperature of the air on your skin?
Smell the sweet aromas.
What are the tastes?
With all your senses, experience this place.
You feel so peaceful, safe and comfortable.

With an individual, one-on-one experience, you may wish to discuss the client's favorite place of peace and safety before the imagery, and then take them there in your induction. This type of induction works extremely well with children. A child's imagination takes them to some amazing and magical places.

PARADOXICAL INTENTION

This type of induction works wonders with a client who is extremely tense. Most of the time they might not even feel the tension, it's just normal. It's normal to hold their shoulders up to their ears. But when you invite them to tense even further and then relax, they can feel the difference. Suggest sequentially tightening and tensing all the muscles in the body. Tighter and tighter, and then relax. The body can only hold tension for just so long.

Progressively working down the body, start with the face. This is the easiest place to begin since the smallest muscles in the body are around the eyes. Tensing and squinting the eyes shut, tensing up the jaw muscles, squeezing up the face, pulling up the shoulders, clenching the fists, pulling in the belly, tightening the thighs and legs, which are the longest and largest muscles in the body, and then ending with curling up the toes.

Get comfortable with your induction. Remember, the primary purpose of any induction is relaxing you, the therapist. The client will naturally start to entrain to your rhythm, your cadence, your relaxation. Create this induction in your own words, so it flows naturally and effortlessly, incorporating long pauses; plenty of time for the client to see, feel and sense the process.

Note that we use the word 'invite' in the induction. This is such a wonderful invitation for the client to see whatever they want and create what their unconscious needs. Often a command of, "You will see this," or "I want you to see that," may bring out the rebellious part of the client, who may not wish to be told what to see or feel.

Again, we refer to the Appendix, which includes four suggested inductions. We have included 'The Body of Color', 'The White Light', and the 'Place of Peace'. Included also is the 'Paradoxical Intention' induction, which further expands into a full imagery experience. This particular imagery was originally created for teenagers dealing with stress and anxiety. Anxiety has become an epidemic in our teen population as they try to cope with all the pressures of their hi-tech world. However, this script could be modified easily to use with adults with the same efficacy.

These scripts are merely suggestions and we highly recommend that you create your own inductions, using your own words. But use whatever we have provided as a springboard to your own creativity.

SUGGESTED CHAPTER STUDY

- Create and get comfortable with at least two inductions you can use with your clients. Make them your own, using your own words and phrasing. Keep them simple and try to stimulate all the senses: to see, to feel, to touch, to smell, to taste. For example, "See the vibrant color orange, you can almost taste it." This can bring about a host of sensory stimulation. Also, remember, the induction is for relaxing both you and the client. As you start to naturally relax, the client will entrain to you.

- Become familiar with at least two different pieces of music, making sure they are seamless for the entire imagery experience. No copyright permission is ever required for any music you use in a private session. Only if you record an imagery for sale or distribution would you be required to pay a royalty.

CHAPTER FOUR

WHY INTRAPERSONAL IMAGERY

We call our version of guided imagery IntraPersonal Imagery – The Journey into Self – because we believe that the most important purpose of imagery is to provide individual opportunity to explore the depths of both physical and emotional healing. This personal journey is the key ingredient of our work. Yes, we want to provide you with skills and information to better prepare you to be a great Guided Imagery Therapist, but that can't be done without first experiencing the healing power of imagery for yourself. This is a journey that can change your life, heal your body and transform your mind and ways of being. Without your own personal experience, you would find it difficult to believe in or fully understand the experiences of your clients.

The six goals in our training and therapy with clients include:

DIAGNOSIS

IntraPersonal Imagery is a relaxation method that enables the client to obtain instant access to feelings and the unconscious, by-passing that censor we call the brain or the conscious mind. Trauma and pain can be identified, truth can be revealed about the past, false belief systems are clarified, all without judgment.

Let's define the term 'judgment', which has both positive and negative connotations. When we receive information about us that we perceive will put us in a bad light, either to self or others, the first tendency is often to defend against this information, deny it or even repress it.

The implication is to admit we did something wrong or to having a bad character. We can all do bad things, or have something bad happen to us, but that is not automatically a description of our character. Good people often do things they are embarrassed about or that go against their values and can still have good character. We are not perfect people and good people can do bad things. Bad people often do good things.

Being without judgment or withholding judgment stands as one of the strongest principles of our work. Whatever behavior we judge harshly about ourselves, the more our need is to ignore it or defend ourselves against it. By withholding judgment about being a good or bad person, we are then free to experience and explore all the circumstances and issues of our past and look at it all as just information that is essential to understanding what happened and why. We need to understand our past for the purpose of clarification and healing. There is no bad truth; there is no good truth either. Truth just is.

A SAFE PLACE

A safe place with a caring therapist enables the client to experience pain, discomfort and embarrassment and not be destroyed by it. Giving both permission and safety to freely experience any and all feelings is the beginning of healing.

UNDERSTAND CAUSE AND EFFECT

"Why me? Why this? Why now?" Ever ask those questions, perhaps even today, usually in an angry and bitter voice? They are really good questions. What is the meaning of the various experiences of our life? What is the message or learning that we are to receive? How can we reconcile the conflicts between our many sub-personalities, or parts of us, that we manage to externalize into outside relationships?

Most of our conflicts with others are extensions of inner conflicts; parts of us or sub-personalities we haven't acknowledged, understood or resolved within ourselves. A sub-personality could be, for example, our anger or our fear. When we are feeling excessive rage, it's as though the angry person inside just takes over and the other parts, such as logic or fear of consequences, go out the window.

ACCEPTANCE AND FORGIVENESS

Because there is no judgment, there can be an acceptance of reality, a seeing without distortion or denial, a forgiveness of self and others. Forgiveness does not imply condoning hurtful or unacceptable behavior; it is rather a releasing of the issue or trauma, choosing not to let it go on affecting our life. To not forgive is to give total power over the rest of our life to the one who injured us. Unresolved anger has two options, find a scapegoat to take it out on or go inside and take it out on the person who is holding this anger, which is us, and we remain a victim.

As quoted in *The Dance of Deception*, a groundbreaking book published by Dr. Harriet Lerner in 1989, *While anger deserves our attention and respect, we still learn to silence our anger, to deny it entirely, or to vent it in a way that leaves us feeling helpless and powerless. We remain a victim as long as we are waiting for the perpetrator to say they're sorry.*

HEALING

Healing can be both physical and emotional; changing perceptions and beliefs that have crippled us. Sometimes reliving a traumatic experience and just getting new information and new understanding about the event, often removes the trauma. As an example, a client believes his father beat him because he hated him and wished he had never been born. In an imagery, taking the client back to one of those beatings, the father apologizes and explains he was also beaten as a child and felt this was the only way he knew how to show love and correct the child.

The incident hasn't changed, but the trauma connected to the incident can be healed with new understanding of the father's motives. With this new information, forgiving the father is possible. We can forgive the father, without forgiving the actions. This can bring a flood of good feelings back about dad and stimulate a host of positive chemicals throughout the body that boosts the immune system and enables a natural healing. We can't change what has happened to us. We can't change our history, but we have all the power to change the emotions wrapped around each event that has injured us.

One of the techniques introduced by Edith R. Stauffer in her book, *Unconditional Love and Forgiveness,* is writing down all the people who have hurt us in some way. In a form of imagery, she invites us to visualize each person, state how they injured us and then re-frame each event with positive statements of, "You did this, but I wish you had done it differently," finishing each sentence with how we would have liked the experience to have unfolded.

Since the brain cannot tell the difference between what's real and what's imagined, this process can indeed begin to heal the past. Dr. Stauffer's theoretical orientation is Psychosynthesis and the work of Roberto Assagioli, M.D, which we will go into detail in Chapter Thirteen.

TRANSFORMATION

Enlightenment and empowerment come when we make contact with the spiritual dimensions of the true inner self and its connection with our higher power or universal truth. Many people are afraid of exploring their unconscious mind because that's where the dark side of us resides. All of our ways of coping with life reside in the unconscious, both desirable and undesirable. The good news is that the intuitive part of our wisdom and power also resides there, too. We will know the truth and the truth will set us free. Know that we and this intuitive part of us are enough for any circumstance or situation.

A WORD ABOUT CARL JUNG

Similarly, Carl Jung defined an imagery experience or visualization to be successful only when the following three components were met:

- Creating a SACRED PLACE, a place where the client feels safe and peaceful.
- Introducing a MAGICAL ENERGY, which could include meeting a spirit guide, a healer, a wise person, a healing temple, or as simple as seeing a symbol of the pain, physical or emotional.
- Providing a TRANSFORMATIONAL RITUAL, which affords the client the opportunity to change or heal, which is the objective of the whole experience. Perhaps a ritual of flushing the body with a magic solution, the re-parenting of the wounded child or meeting the 'remembered well you'; whatever situation is created to transform the client. Many times, at the end of an imagery to heal the wounded child within, the suggestion is made to have a sacred ceremony of adopting this child.

Tapping into the unconscious indeed brings about personal truth. By separating from our strength, which includes all our defense mechanisms of survival, repression and even denial, we truly can empower ourselves with courage, which is the true authenticity of who we are. Years ago we found this poem, which says it so beautifully.

STRENGTH AND COURAGE

It takes strength to be firm
It takes courage to be gentle

It takes strength to stand guard
It takes courage to let down your guard

It takes strength to conquer
It takes courage to surrender

It takes strength to be certain
It takes courage to have doubt

It takes strength to fit in
It takes courage to stand out

It takes strength to feel a friend's pain
It takes courage to feel your own pain

It takes strength to hide your own pains
It takes courage to show them

It takes strength to endure abuse
It takes courage to stop it

It takes strength to stand alone
It takes courage to lean on another

It takes strength to love
It takes courage to be loved

It takes strength to survive
It takes courage to live

Author unknown

SUGGESTED CHAPTER STUDY

- Incorporating these six goals and the three components of Jung, create an imagery script to meet a sub-personality within.

- In the example of the client who was beaten by his father, we unfolded the experience where the father apologized and was remorseful. How would you proceed if you were the therapist and dad was defensive and would not take responsibility for his actions? Not sure? Keep reading.

CHAPTER FIVE

THE WORK OF THE PIONEERS

Two highly regarded imagery therapists from our past, Dr. Robert DeSoille and Dr. Hanscarl Leuner, used universal symbols extensively with their clients, and according to DeSoille, *These symbols could reveal the nature of the trauma and alleviate symptoms rapidly.*

Desoille called his type of imagery the *Directed Daydream* and his therapy was essentially Jungian in character with a goal to uncover and resolve the patient's habitual patterns and distortions. He developed six themes for starting therapy that would tend to reveal the various struggles of life we all encounter and thereby provide a diagnosis for future therapeutic work. In essence we could say that rather than have the client tell him what the current issues might be, DeSoille preferred to go directly to these universal symbols and allow them to reveal the problems and even begin the process of correction and change along the way.

Quoting DeSoille directly from lectures he presented in 1965, he writes the following: *We are now prepared to discuss the basis for choosing the starting images on which the directed daydreams are to be constructed, most obviously, man must confront himself; and subsequently, he must come to terms with others. This means that in order to understand the patient, it behooves us to ask him about himself and to explore his attitudes toward both men and women. However, if this inquiry were conducted in conventional language, it would tell us very little, if anything at all. Therefore it must be conducted in a symbolic language, the universal language of dreams. Most often, the patient will answer our questions with visual images, but sometimes auditory and even olfactory sensations will arise. In any case, they should all be treated as symbols.*

He goes on to explain that the advantage of a symbolic mode of expression is that it provides the client with the greatest possible freedom of expression because even though the client is describing his imagery in conventional language, he is not aware of its true meaning. Therefore, he feels no need to control the expression of feelings he is experiencing in the imagery or directed daydream. In other words, there is less, or no need, for judgment of what he is experiencing. Here are the six themes that DeSoille used as a starting point for his treatment sessions:

THE SWORD AND THE VASE

The purpose, according to DeSoille, is confronting one's more obvious characteristics. Interesting enough, he would use the sword only for the man and the vase only for the woman. In our certification program, we do a similar imagery and we simply call this our masculinity and femininity. Since everyone has both characteristics within them, we use both the sword and the vase with everyone.

We obviously live in a different world and culture than in the 1960's when DeSoille was developing his therapies. Today both sexes are more comfortable, are being more aware of and are talking about both sides of their nature. Just by exploring the type of sword and vase, the descriptions and how each symbol felt about each other, we can learn extensively how we relate to our world and ourselves. We also ask the sword and vase to make statements to each other, which will tell us if they admire and get along well with each other. Or perhaps, they are in conflict; the conflict between us is the conflict within me.

THE OCEAN

DeSoille calls this confronting one's more suppressed characteristics and for both sexes a descent into the depths of the ocean, which can also be seen as the great unconscious mind.

THE WITCH OR A SORCERESS

A decent into a cave to come to terms with mother.

THE WIZARD OR MAGICIAN

A decent into a cave to come to terms with father. Actually, for both sexes, he wants you first of all to deal with the parent of the opposite sex and in the second imagery deal with the parent of the same sex.

THE CAVE OF THE FABLED DRAGON

This is the journey of coming to terms with societal constraints. Remember, the job description of our parents is to teach us right from wrong, morals and standards, acceptable behavior in the world. Society is the larger version of parent, and sets the ultimate standard. In both cases, the job description of the child is to challenge these authorities, test limits, and find their own beliefs and values to live by.

THE OEDIPAL SITUATION AND THE CASTLE OF SLEEPING BEAUTY

There are many stories or versions of *Sleeping Beauty*, all with the same theme. A young princess is the favorite delight of her father, the king. There is usually a jealous step-mother, who fears this love relationship and sees the daughter as a threat to her own power with the king. And so, she creates a potion or poison to drug the young girl and put her in a long sleep or coma. The grieving king puts his daughter's body on public display. Years later, when she arrives at the stage of her teens, a young visiting prince comes, sees her, and bewitched by her beauty, kisses her. She awakens and they fall in love.

This is a classical description of Freud's theory of childhood development. Between three and five years of age, each child goes through a stage of desiring to have sex and marry the parent of the opposite sex. The powerful parents each deny the child this sexually inappropriate relationship, and with some trauma, the child gives up this desire to marry their parents and the trauma and disappointment throws them into a latency period of about ten years or so. At this point puberty arrives and they are thrust into their sexual urges once again. Read the story again and you will see how it co-ordinates with Freud's theory.

Using the sword as an example of what an imagery might look like for interpretation, DeSoille suggests, *One person will visualize a substantial weapon, another will see an ornate ceremonial sword, while a third might picture a blade without a handle. Still another might imagine a long thin blade with a handle at each end, making it useless as a weapon. And as a final example, representing an extreme in the range of possible responses, a patient might be able to image only a photograph of a sword.*

Dr. Hanscarl Leuner created *Guided Affective Imagery* in 1948. 'Affect' has to do with emotions, so it is essentially guided emotional imagery. He was psychoanalytically oriented, in line with Freud, and considered his approach, *As a controlled regression of the ego to earlier emotional levels and ways of functioning.* Leuner proceeds on the assumption of the existence of unconscious drive impulses, motivations and defense processes revealed by dream symbols. It is easy to see that both Freud and Jung had similar approaches to uncovering the past as a way of healing the present.

Leuner also had a basic level of imagery that he considered to be, *A superior, short therapy that closed the gap between symptom-centered procedures and the great psychoanalytic cure.* 'Symptom-centered procedures' would be the types of therapy that focus on removing the symptom rather than seeking the cause. All behavioral modification approaches, such as Gestalt therapy, and all the behavioral therapies, would be examples of this approach. On the other hand, the great psychoanalytic cure is, of course, Freud and the others who practice what is often called *Depth Psychology*, and believe that going back to the original cause from childhood and making corrections is the only way to heal the symptoms or behavior.

THE MEADOW

Leuner always began with a meadow motif. In his own words, he considered the meadow, *A giving attitude toward the client, allowing him spontaneous space to fulfill his own wishes.* He used this as a stage for current conflictual projections. We add here that our further view of the meadow represents unconditional mother love, which is highly correlated with Leuner's view. Leuner felt that a description of the meadow itself could be a direct correlation with the client's ability to receive this giving attitude or any unconditional love given as a child. Was it large or small, lush or bare, rigid or open? How was the weather?

From our point of view, the larger, more lush and beautiful the meadow and the weather, the more unconditional love the person received as a child from mother or even mothering from others. In using the meadow motif in our work, we have provided this setting with thousands of students and clients and found that most of them would have a pleasant or positive experience of the meadow, even though many of them did not have an exceptionally good or unconditional loving experience as a child, especially from mother. It seems that the best answer to why this might be is that most of us, even with poor mothering as a child, somewhere along the path of becoming an adult, found a lot of love and support from surrogate mothers or were able to give it to ourselves or at least would be open to receive a form of unconditional love from someone who offered it.

A small, barren or average meadow would show different aspects of childhood experiences. A divided meadow, half lush and half overgrown with weeds or marshland, might reveal that the client had two mothers, perhaps one being a step-mother. One was seen as good and the other bad, or the actual mother might play both roles and it was never known which one to expect. A snake or bull in the meadow might be a sibling or father figure that was competing for mother's love. We feel that adding the dimension of unconditional mother love to Leuner's giving attitude towards the client can bring a more focused beginning to a meadow experience at the first stages of imagery.

A BROOK OR STREAM

The second imagery of his basic level would be to find a brook or stream of water in the meadow. He would invite his client to choose to walk or swim upstream or downstream in the brook. Which would you choose? Would you choose to go upstream or downstream?

People who choose to go downstream generally state that it would be easier and they would want to flow with the water instead of the hard work of swimming upstream, against the current. Those who choose to go upstream state that they wish to go to the source. Leuner would eventually take them in both directions regardless of where they choose to begin, but is quick to point out that downstream is not as simple as it suggests. Downhill feeds into the ocean, a long journey, and will encounter many obstacles along the way: dams, rapids, trees and rocks to name a few. Going upstream is definitely Leuner's choice for a healing, 'good mother' experience.

When asked the source of water, it is surprising how many of our students will answer that it is rain that provides the source of our water, but it's not. We hear much about the lack of rain or draught conditions that are costing us a loss of water supply on the earth, but the original source of water is from deep within the earth.

Leuner would take the client upstream to the original source of the brook and expect them to find a place where there was a flow of water coming spontaneously from the earth. Beneath this waterfall, find a pond. He would invite the client to go into the pool of water. There, he would instruct the client to drink this healing fluid, mother's milk, to provide nourishment and love. If there were bruises or physical pain, he would encourage rubbing the fluid on those places for a healing experience. Going downstream would enable the client to deal with the many obstacles and issues of their life, and work through them to bring forth a transformation and healing of the parts not functioning well. This could take many imageries, as you might well imagine.

In our training, we call this liquid or fluid, the magic or healing solution. Since Leuner's time, it has been scientifically proven that there is not a chemical in the pharmacy that the body cannot replicate and better, with no side effects and contraindications. This magic solution can flush away poisons and toxins, alleviate pain and discomfort. Similar to the efficacy of the placebo effect, if we believe we can create this elixir, the body will respond. And, it does!

Right now, imagine that you're holding a spray bottle filled with this solution, all the chemicals from your own body to heal any pains or aches. What color is it? How do you feel just holding this bottle? We invite you right now to put the book down and imagine yourself spraying any part of your body that may hold tension or discomfort. Allow this solution to flush away any pain. How does that feel? We incorporate this in many of our imageries; a marvelous tool in both physical and emotional healing.

THE MOUNTAIN

The third imagery would be to observe a mountain from the meadow, a universal symbol of father. Observe it from a distance. What are the feelings about the mountain? Is it approachable or dangerous? It's the mastering of a task. Much like the mythical journey talked about by Joseph Campbell, 'go find your father'; find where we come from, our heritage, and who we are. Leuner always finishes with a descent from the mountain and expects the meadow to be improved when the client returns, which symbolizes that a healing took place.

THE HOUSE

The fourth imagery is seeing and entering a house, also in the meadow, which is explored as a symbol of the person. Here the client would project all his fears and wishes about himself. On the one hand, if he visualizes a castle, he may thereby demonstrate that he has very ambitious and grandiose expectations from life. On the other hand, if only a small hut can be visualized, this may indicate a serious lack of self-esteem.

In our use of 'The House' imagery, we believe each room represents a different part or aspect of self. The living room tends to represent the way we show ourselves to the outside world. Use 'tends to' in all of these; nothing is absolute. The dining room tends to represent the way we entertain and nourish others. The kitchen is where we nourish self or were nourished as a child. The bedroom represents our sensuality, creativity and sexuality. The bathroom tends to represent our private side, how we take care of ourselves, our hygiene and our inner self image in our nakedness. Even suggesting a reflection of self in a mirror in the bathroom can be quite revealing.

Leuner says to look at the food that is stored in the pantry and refrigerator. He suggests paying attention to single or double beds and the contents of the closets. Leuner's writes, *A young female patient may find her own clothes stored in close proximity to her father's.* He's a Freudian, after all. Of further interest to Leuner is the cellar and attic. They often contain reminders of one's childhood such as toys or pictures.

In doing this imagery in our seminars, we will generally ask to find something in the attic that seems important, bring it downstairs and place it in one of the rooms. This is something from the past that needs to be worked through, and where it is placed can have significance. For example, say a client brought a family photo album down from the attic and placed it on the dining room table. What would be your interpretation of that?

We also ask the client to go outside and view the house when finished with all the rooms, and provide the opportunity to change it in any way they would like. You could also ask what room they liked the best in the house and what room was liked least and then describe what caused them to have these feelings. Note in the Appendix, we have included the actual script for our rendition of 'The House' Imagery. This can be a great first imagery experience to do with a client and as you can see, can be extremely revealing and diagnostic.

THE EDGE OF THE WOODS

The fifth imagery in Leuner's basic level of experiences invites the client to move from the meadow to the edge of the woods or forest. Look into the darkness to allow symbolic figures to come forth. He expects figures from fairy tales, wild animals, evil, or perhaps friendly, figures to emerge. He interprets these figures both subjectively and objectively, which means that subjectively, all the figures represent various sub-personalities of the client, and objectively as all the figures represent someone or something in the outside world, such as people or situations. He wants the client to bring these unfinished aspects or symbols out of the darkness, into the light of day, nourish and even satiate them and hopefully, reconcile with them.

This is a very strong value of ours, as well. We see our job as helping the client to reconcile and make peace with all the various parts of self and the outside world. The dark side of self is not evil or the enemy. Much of our strength and power is located in what we refer to as the dark side. We need that strength for leadership and appropriate use of power to contact the good authority within us. Our job is the bring it out of the darkness of the unconscious, into the light of day, find the true need and purpose of the sub-personality, meet that need so that it begins to function in a more appropriate fashion. This brings it into full harmony and balance within us. More on this later.

An added word on Leuner, the explanation above was taken from his book, *Guided Affective Imagery*, published in 1948. In our syllabus, which is a 600-page compilation of articles and material about imagery provided to our students and graduates, there is a lecture presented by Leuner at the New Jersey Neuropsychiatric Institute, Princeton, NJ in 1966. In that paper he describes ten different imageries or levels, however, we are staying with his five basic levels for reference here.

FREUD AND JUNG

Since we introduced Leuner and DeSoille as followers of Freud and Jung, indeed a reference is in order about imagery as used by these pioneers. Freud used imagery extensively prior to 1900. His method was to tell the client he was going to place his hand firmly on the client's forehead and then would slowly reduce the pressure. The client was to observe the spontaneous images that appeared as he relaxed the pressure. In rapid succession, various scenes related to the central conflict were seen, usually events from the past in chronological order. One might compare this to using Freud's free association in an imagery setting.

Around 1900, he stopped using imagery, saying, *My therapy consists of wiping away these pictures.* Since he continued to use dream work as the 'royal road to the unconscious', and dream and imagery interpretations are virtually the same, there had to be a difference between the two for Freud.

Freud's theory of child development was based on his beliefs connected to the oedipal complex. Between three and five years of age children go through a stage of desiring sex with the parent of the opposite sex. This came from Freud's clients sharing dreams and experiencing imageries of having sex with their parents. Since the truth of these being real episodes was not acceptable in the society of Vienna at that time in history, Freud explained it as the natural process and fantasy that every child goes through.

The process of maturation is that the parents reject this seduction, the child gives up this conquest and the client becomes 'normal'. Since Freud continued to work with dreams but dropped imagery, our conclusion is that the visuals in imagery were so much more vivid and immediate than in dreams, Freud couldn't talk them out of the belief that the sex really took place.

Jung on the other hand, continued to use imagery throughout his career. He called it *Active Imagination* and stated, *Images have a life of their own and the symbolic events develop according to their own logic, if the conscious reason doesn't interfere.* Jung also said, *The Active Imagination process is superior to dreams in defeating the unconscious and quickening maturation in analysis.* In spite of this belief, Jung was also somewhat afraid of the power of imagery and didn't feel everyone was ready for this direct confrontation with their natural flow of images until later in therapy or after the completion of analysis.

Jung listed six reasons for using imagery:

- When it is obvious the unconscious is overflowing with fantasies.
- To reduce the number of dreams when there are too many.
- When not enough dreams are being remembered.
- When someone feels or seems to be under indefinable influences.
- When adaptation to life has been injured.
- When someone falls in the same hole again and again.

Commenting on the first three, they may seem confusing. If the unconscious is overflowing with fantasies, why would we compound the confusion by adding imagery? Because overflowing with fantasies is a sign that the unconscious is trying to get our attention and feels overwhelmed. Doing a guided imagery is a message to the unconscious that we are listening and open to learn. The imageries will be dealing with the uncovered issues and then there is no longer a need for the fantasy overload.

The same is true of having too many dreams and the result is the same. Think of this like a child who feels neglected and literally drives you crazy, demanding attention. The more he demands, the more you push him away, feeling that the demand is too great and the more you give, the greater the demand will be. Let's say your therapist advises you to give the child thirty minutes a day of your undivided attention and you try it. To your amazement, in two or three days the child stops demanding, since he now feels loved and cared about.

What about having no dreams, or not enough that are remembered? Many people have managed to shut off their dream access and will tell you they are never or rarely aware of dreams. Our experience has been that once they have participated in an imagery, they come back to tell us they had several dreams the very next night. If the unconscious has repressed dreams due to fear of the information, and then the person does an imagery and nothing bad happens as a result of getting in touch with these buried feelings, the person becomes more open and receptive.

So, we might define Jung as an analyst who occasionally used imagery in his work. The difference with DeSoille and Leuner is that they were Guided Imagery Therapists and that was the focus of their entire work. Their analytical training helped prepare them for using imagery. Rather than starting with a long client history to decide a diagnosis for the client, they each used their basic level of imagery to begin the process and went to advanced imageries to reach their diagnostic conclusions. All of their therapy was based on imagery and the interpretations and learning that came out of the imageries.

In our comments about DeSoille and Leuner, we have added how we adapted some of their imageries into IntraPersonal Imagery. When we say we use some of these imageries in our work, we have taken the universal symbols that others have used and created our own original scripts on each subject. Universal symbols are just that and can't be copyrighted.

When facilitating a one-on-one with a client, as practiced by DeSoille and Leuner, there is obviously no script. After a relaxing induction, the client is communicating with the therapist as they are taken on a journey. From that point on, the therapist is following the client, responding to the experience as shared, asking questions, making suggestions with the intent of gathering information vital to the client, and working towards a positive conclusion.

In reviewing the works of DeSoille, Leuner, Freud and Jung, the more contemporary pioneers in the field of imagery include Dr. Emmett Miller, with his groundbreaking research into Psychoneuroimmunology; the mind-body connection. He discovered that thoughts can alter our pathology, and with the use of imagery and positive affirmations, the body can create healing. We also pay tribute to the work of the late Dr. O. Carl Simonton, who introduced imagery for the treatment of cancer. His technique of visualizing 'Pac Man', one of the first video games in the late

1970's, invites patients to literally imagine these 'Pac Man' figures going through their bodies and eating up all the cancer cells.

The tireless research of hundreds of clinicians today is bringing the field of imagery into the legitimacy it deserves as an effective tool in both physical and emotional healing. In particular, recognition must be made to Belleruth Naparstek. Through her incredible work with hospitals and medical centers around the country, she must be considered the driving force in bringing the power of imagery into the forefront as a complementary modality in healing. It's not uncommon today to find her imagery CDs available in local hospitals and other medical facilities.

SUGGESTED CHAPTER STUDY

- Using Leuner's motif of the brook, create a quick imagery experience to journey upstream and find the source. At this source, provide a ritual of healing with the magic solution.

- We discussed the correlation between the story of *Sleeping Beauty* and Freud's theory of childhood development. Many believe that fairy tales from our past are imprinted in our subconscious; that they help create belief systems within us, and in some way shape how our lives will unfold. Think about a story or fairy tales that you really resonated with as a kid and see if there is any correction with your own life story.

- We suggest the book, *Staying Well with Guided Imagery*, by Belleruth Naparstek, as an incredible adjunct to the power of imagery for health and healing.

CHAPTER SIX

CHOOSING A SUBJECT –
THE PRESENTING PROBLEM

When a client comes to therapy, after the general getting acquainted time, the first question asked by the therapist should be, "How can I help you?" That's a way of asking, "What's the discomfort or pain that brings you to see me at this time in your life?"

There are infinite reasons you may hear, but generally they will fit into seven categories:

- A physical problem or ailment
- A prior life trauma or wounded child within
- Marriage or relationship issues
- Anger management
- Fear management
- Anxiety
- Depression

Interestingly enough, the presenting problem given to you by the client may not be the real issue. Here are two examples. The client may say the issue at hand is anxiety, "I need to relax and I can't."

You have two options of approach. As an imagery therapist, you may smile and say, "You've come to the right place. That's what I've been trained to do. We'll do imagery and I'll show you how to relax." A second approach would be to do imagery with the anxious part of the client that has no intention of relaxing and probably sees relaxing as a bad thing to do.

A client might say, "I tend to be a victim in life and want to learn how to be more assertive with others." Again, there are two options. Push the client to take risks, to be more assertive and courageous, which is what the client seems to be asking you to help them with. Or, take the opposite approach and work with the victim. Explore the fear of becoming assertive, and why that's not a desirable characteristic.

The more obvious approach for either of these two examples would be to give the client what they want and what they are asking for. However, this is usually the most difficult to accomplish and comes with a lot of resistance. The issues of being an anxious person or tending to be a victim in life didn't happen overnight. These are life-long issues that perhaps parents and many others have tried to talk them out of with obviously little or no success. Anxiety or being a victim has won every battle to not change.

Honor that part of the client that doesn't want to change and find out why. Don't try to overcome reluctance or remove an obstacle until you have explored its reasons for being there. This is very important. Every symptom is a part of self, protecting us from behavior that the symptom perceives as a more painful result. Talking to the resistant part of the client may give you the real reasons for not changing. "If I'm not anxious and alert, I'll be lazy and depressed or not try hard enough or even be taken advantage of and hurt. If I am assertive that means being a bully like my father and hurting people, and no one will like me if I act that way." That's good information. The true issue is usually the reason for not changing, rather than the need to change.

You will be hearing this many times in the book, but we'll start with it now. Every sub-personality within us is good at its core, with good intent to protect us from emotional pain. Our goal is always to help make peace with each and every part, if they are willing to cooperate. Never see these symptoms or parts as enemies needing to be destroyed. We really can't destroy a part of ourselves, even if we try. Let's find the true need of each sub-personality, use imagery to bring it to the light of day, and then, meet that need to provide an opportunity for change and growth.

Whether you consider yourself a healer or therapist, nurse or health practitioner, your job is not to fix or change people or even solve their problems, even when you are expected to and in some cases, demanded to. Your job is to ask the right questions to explore the reasons why they don't change. Honor and listen to the parts that resist change; the self that is in conflict. Honoring and listening brings understanding and clarity. Demanding change, or else, only brings resistance. Giving permission not to change disarms resistance and can remove guilt and blame.

Often, giving permission to not change reveals more hidden belief systems imposed by others. A client might say, "My father told me if I wasn't an A student, I'd be a loser, so if I try hard and fail to get A's, then dad is right, I'm a loser. If I try hard and succeed in getting A's, then dad is right and I've given him control over my life. The only way I can win or be my own person is to not let dad win, and not get A's. My defense is that A's are not important to me and I'm rejecting dad's stupid values. I could get A's if I wanted to."

Let's stop for a moment and do a brief imagery. The issue is anxiety and the need to be calm. As you slowly read the words, let anything happen that wants to happen. After each sentence take a moment to just see, feel and experience and then go to the next.

QUICK IMAGERY
A ROOM CALLED ANXIETY

See yourself standing in a room called ANXIETY. Just be there, slowly look around the room and be aware of what you see and feel.

Where in your body do you feel the anxiety?

What is the best part of being anxious?

What does being anxious help you accomplish?

What does it keep you from doing?

Through a glass partition you see an adjoining room called CALM, go closer and see this room.

How is this room similar or different than the one you're in right now?

Imagine yourself being in that room called CALM. How do you feel there?

What do you like best about that feeling?

What do you like least about that feeling?

Now, slowly and deliberately, let yourself come back to this room.

We suggest that you get a pen and some paper before you go on with your reading and take some time to write down your imagery experience. Be very aware of all the feelings that came up. Using the words of the imagery to remind you, describe the room called anxiety and how you felt there. Write about the complete experience. Remember, we are just gathering information. Nothing in your experience should be considered good or bad, its just information.

Most people, anxious or not, tend to see a lot of chaos in a room of anxiety. Where you feel it in your body is probably the place where you hold those feelings of anxiety and stress most of the time. Stomach, lower back or neck and shoulders are common areas. Have you been aware of this before? The best part of being anxious for most people is that it creates an instant alertness to danger and a call to action. It helps us to defend ourselves. The question, "What does it keep me from doing?" is generally answered with, "I felt too overwhelmed to function." What were your feelings?

How was the room called calm different or similar to the first room? Did you go there and how did you respond to the calm room?

For most people this peaceful place looks very different and feels wonderful. For people who tend to feel anxious most of the time, they may feel uncomfortable with calm and don't want to go or stay there too long. They may love the colors and serenity, but they feel bored or lazy after a time. A certain amount of tension seems to be necessary and appropriate for alertness and staying attentive. What did this brief exercise of imagery teach you about yourself? What surprised you the most?

SYMBOLS

At the beginning of this chapter, we mentioned there are generally seven different reasons or issues why a client would seek out the experience of guided imagery. There is another approach to beginning therapy; the use of universal symbols to discover the underlying causes and issues of the client. As imagery practitioners, the use of symbols is the most exciting reason of all to delve into the subconscious.

There are two types of symbols to consider, and as we mentioned previously, a universal symbol is one that tends to mean the same to all people, regardless of sex, age, culture or history. Students often ask us, "Who decides what these symbols mean and how do we know they mean the same to everyone?" Those who study mythology, dreams and history have found that symbols tend to come up over and over with the same general meaning for all of us. Joseph Campbell, the great mythologist, spent his life devoted to seeing the threads of meaning and metaphor in stories, myths and fairytales throughout history. These common themes tell the story of our commonality and our belonging, and are imprinted in our subconscious.

IN THE TELLING

Each of us has a different story
each of us is unique
in this singular beauty
we all find our worth
our meaning

But in the telling of
our special tales
we find the thread
that is woven into
the fabric of the whole

We find the sameness
that makes us feel
we belong

The second type of symbol is the particular; that a symbol means something uniquely personal to each individual. How we describe a symbol in a dream or imagery, what we feel it means to us, whether we like it or not and what we feel it's telling us, is far more important than the universal meaning. These feelings about the experience or symbol are coming from deep within and need to be honored first and foremost.

Freud had a slightly different way of dealing with this. If a client agreed with his interpretation, it was correct. If the client disagreed, they were resisting the truth and not yet ready to deal with this information. We agree with Freud partially in that there are people who are very resistant to hearing or seeing information that they can't or won't accept about themselves. Our experience has been that this is less threatening in the safe and relaxed place of imagery. Even if this resistance happens in an imagery, just know that even though this is good information for both the client the therapist, you don't have to pursue it now.

Our approach to this issue is to explore with the client first, to discover all the information we can get about the imagery and the client's descriptions and feelings about the various symbols. Then and only then do we reveal the universal meaning. Again, remember the particular symbol and the client's impression about it are more important than the universal meaning, however adding the universal truth after the particular meaning is discussed can add some deeper and richer interpretation.

There are many wonderful reference books available on symbols and metaphor. Any good dream dictionary is a great place to start. We recommend the work of Ted Andrews in his three books, *Animal-Wise, Animal-Speak* and *Nature-Speak.* We also recommend the books, *Feelings Buried Alive Never Die,* by Karol Truman and the classic, *You Can Heal Your Life,* by Louise Hay. Both are great reference for symbolism associated with the body and physical imbalance.

It is often surprising what the books say and how the universal meaning supports or adds to what the client has shared, even when they had no previous knowledge of that particular animal or symbol. This brings more understanding to the client, as well as the therapist, that these truths are somehow encoded in our subconscious and tend to validate that the symbols truly do have universal meaning.

One final note, in discussing with the client the universal meaning of any symbol or the interpretation you may find in a reference book, always use the words 'tends to'. For example, a client may see a deer that represents a part of him. He may be repelled by the vulnerability and defenselessness of the animal. Only after exploring his interpretations, you may share with him the universal meaning.

According to Ted Andrews, *The deer tends to represent a time to be gentle with yourself and an opportunity to express gentle love that will open new doors of adventure.* Always ask the client, "How do you resonate with that interpretation?" It's uncanny, however, how accurate these universal symbols and metaphors can be, and can bring a new insight or perspective.

Through the years, after facilitating hundreds of imageries with clients and hearing about their various symbols, we have researched and compiled our own directory of universal symbols, including the most common animals, the symbolism of earth elements, colors, flowers, foods, numbers, you name it. This directory is included in the Appendix.

In looking up any symptom or physical problem for yourself or your client in this Appendix, please bear in mind, the interpretations are merely suggestions of possible meanings and clues of what the body may be trying to tell us. Never define a person by their disease and symptom. Symptoms are a marvelous way of listening to the body. The problem can be a message of what needs to be examined. The body carries muscle memory, and often, the physical problem can be the beginning of letting go of old traumas or memories from the past. The Appendix includes excerpts from Louise L. Hay's book, *You Can Heal Your Life*, as well as *Feelings Buried Alive Never Die*, by Karol Truman. In imagery, having a dialogue with an animal that represents the pain or imbalance can be a marvelous springboard to finding resolution and healing. The possible metaphors could provide some possible probative questions to ask the animal along the way.

SUGGESTED CHAPTER STUDY

- We used the example of a client's need to be more assertive. In an imagery, talk to the client's courageous part and also talk to the victim. Similarly, if a client came with issues of abandonment, what two parts, or sub-personalities, could you address and dialogue with?

- Incorporating your above answer, create a simple imagery, similar to 'A Room Called Anxiety', giving a client the experience of these two sub-personalities.

CHAPTER SEVEN

WHERE TO BEGIN THE IMAGERY

There are many places you can begin a guided imagery depending, of course, on both the therapist's as well as the client's intent. If this is your first imagery with someone and the concept of imagery is new to your client, you would probably want to do a simple, non-threatening, relaxation to provide the most peaceful and positive first experience. We suggest providing an induction that would allow them to choose a safe and relaxing place to be, perhaps a meadow, a beach, wherever. Always check with the client first to find if there are any places the client would not feel safe, such as, "I almost drowned in the ocean once." Or, as a pilot client once said, "A mountain top is not a pilot's best friend; mountains are the enemy." As the therapist, find that safe and relaxing place and just keep them exploring and sharing all the sights, sounds, smells and tastes that are available.

Demonstrating how relaxing and peaceful imagery can be, how caring, supportive and non-judgmental you, the therapist can be, is a beautiful way to start. Before you begin, you might even tell the client that your goal is just to give them a quiet and peaceful experience, and not jump right into whatever their issues might be. That can come later. This is the beginning of trust between therapist and client. After that first positive experience, you and your client are ready for that marvelous journey of imagery. You've established the issue and reviewed the intent and goals of the client, you feel confident about providing a relaxing induction, but what then? Where do you begin or set the stage, if you will, to provide an experience that will address the issue?

A PLACE CAN SYMBOLIZE AN ISSUE

Let's go back to our original imagery in Chapter Six, 'A Room Called Anxiety'. The client's issue was anxiety so they were taken to a room with that name. You would expect the client to experience a room that would provoke feelings of anxiety, chaos, even threatening. Other places that could illicit these feelings could be a deep cave or any dark place. Suggesting that it's too dark to see creates the unknown, which is probably the greatest cause of fear.

Our first goal is to allow the client to be in the fear or pain, without judgment, and give them some time to just experience it. Without putting up a defense or running away affords the client the opportunity to face the fear or pain without anything bad happening, and with no negative consequences. This is the first step in realizing the situation they're in is not as bad as they expected it to be, and they'll be ok.

From the room called anxiety, we later offered a second room named calm. Pairs of opposites are often revealing. The calm room brings a sense of peace, protection or safety, but most of us can only stay in total peace for a short time, then we get bored. Excessive fear or calm can be too extreme. A client may come to a new insight that, "Chaos and fear can wear me out and calm doesn't give me enough to do." The anxious person can move out of the extreme, closer to center. And the calm one, who is afraid of responsibility, moving closer to center, can bring a little tension and excitement. Honoring the extremes or polarities can bring them into balance.

THE BODY

The body is one of the easiest places to deal with a symptom, a pain, or a situation. Whether we know it or not, all of us carry both physical and emotional pain in various parts of our bodies. Even a trauma caused by an accident or an illness will hold emotional pain connected to that situation. Let's do another imagery to explain this. Slowly read the words, let anything happen that wants to happen. Remember there's no right way or wrong way to do this. And, there's no judgment, so there's not a good thing or a bad thing to see. It's just information; good information.

QUICK IMAGERY
FIND YOUR MOTHER

Where does your mother reside in your body?

Scan your body to find your mother.

How do you feel about her being in that particular place in your body?

Ask her why she chose that place to be. Wait for her answer.

Look at her face, what emotion do you see?

How would you feel if you were asked to gently remove her and place her on a shelf nearby?

Slowly come back to this room.

Now take a moment to write down what you saw and how you felt. Usually mother is found in a particular part of the body that they wish to control: your genitals, perhaps to control your sexuality, your throat to control what you say, or your brain to control your thoughts or beliefs. You get the picture. In most situations people tend to see the negative side of mother that is trying to control them in some way. In some cases, they see the positive, and may say, "She's in my heart, exactly where I want her to be." Sometimes we're more precise in the imagery and ask to find the negative side of mother in the body.

Asking you to remove your mother is not asking you to reject her. It is asking you to take your body back. Your body, mind and emotions are your responsibility. Put mom on a shelf. You can come and visit her as often as you like, work out your differences and literally change the relationship. Can you think of a few more things you can look for in your body? Where in your body do you hold your job, your marriage, fear, anger, various pains or symptoms?

A WORD ABOUT STRUCTURE AND GOALS

We will provide you with a simple structure that you can use for all imageries to deal with any symptom, issue, pain or problem. This structure will provide direction, concrete steps, goals and intent of how you can take any situation and move it from the position of being an irresolvable problem, to having the ability to talk to the problem, learn what the issues are, negotiate and make peace with it. Thus, we can turn a previously irresolvable problem into an asset and new way of functioning.

Whether it's a group imagery, which requires a fully prepared script and the client silently experiences the imagery, or a one-on-one experience, we will provide you with many ways and places to take clients as a beginning point to start an imagery. In the one-on-one, first you do an induction and then provide a starting point, such as, "Where do you find your mother in your body?" or perhaps, "You find yourself in a room called anxiety." After that you can't follow a script. You will be interacting verbally with the client, who will be describing what they are seeing and are experiencing. Your job at this point is to follow the client and where they lead you, even if that is not where you intended to go. Trust the client.

Your job is to ask questions for more information about the experience and perhaps offer options and suggestions:

- How would you feel about going through that door?
- Talk about your fear.
- Where do you feel the fear in your body?
- What does that fear feel like?
- What does that fear look like?

- What would you like to do now?
- What is happening now?

Remember Jung's definition of imagery, *It has a life of its own and will provide a total life experience on its own.* If the client's conscious mind doesn't interfere and respond with, for example, "I don't want to see a cartoon character, that's too silly," encourage the client to find out what the cartoon wants to tell us, without passing judgment. Your non-judgmental interaction will aid in the story, as long as you are supporting the client's experience, to trust the imagery itself. If your intent is for the client to go through a door and see a certain person and the client goes in a totally different direction, and you keep trying to get them back on your track with your intent, you're missing the point.

For both group and one-on-one, the following goals should always be foremost in the imagery experience:

- Get as much information as you can, especially from the negative sources you are dealing with.
- Honor both the client and the symptom as to their needs.
- Provide opportunity for the client to understand and find clarity about the differences between them.
- Provide possible reconciliation between the client and the problem.
- End on a positive note for your client, even if the best you can say is, "We have learned a lot today and obviously we have a lot more work to do, but this is a good place to end for now."

In doing a group imagery, you are at a disadvantage not knowing if the above goals were met, however, creating rich situations, asking probing questions and allowing pauses in your delivery to make sure the client has sufficient time to process, will help provide a meaningful experience. And, the dialogue with the client after the imagery becomes the barometer of your success in meeting the goals. In many group imageries, it becomes clear in the discussion after the imagery is completed, individuals often don't follow the script and are having a totally different experience than the therapist intended. Have they done it wrong by following their own story? Of course not.

Occasionally, in the discussion after a group imagery, a student will say something like, "That was incredible when you told us to see that flying horse and go for a ride." We never made that suggestion. Their imagery, as Jung would say, had a life of its own, and they were following their own mythic story. Also, if something comes up in the post imagery discussion that needs further clarification or closure, you can always take them back into the imagery. Since, as we mentioned previously, the brain needs about 15 minutes to fully return to the Beta, awake state, it takes just a few comments of induction to get them back into the imagery.

In doing our certification programs, participants experience all the imageries silently, with time after to discuss and interpret. One of the imageries we did included a ritual of sorts where all the people from your life gather around to celebrate you. One student came out of the experience quite emotional with tears rolling down her face. We asked immediately what she was feeling and she shared that in the imagery, she saw all her family, including her brother, who had died suddenly a few years ago. She said it was wonderful to see him again. She explained that she never got an opportunity to say good bye to him before he died.

We asked her permission to take her back into imagery, and invited her to be in that same ritual and find her brother. This time we were dialoguing and she told us how wonderful it was to see him again. We asked her, "What would you like to say to your brother?" Her words were so powerful and then, we asked if her brother had anything to say to her. And through her tears, she told us what he said; such beautiful words of love and joy, an incredible process of closure.

A DREAM

A dream is a wonderful way to begin an imagery for many reasons. The client can share the dream. You might ask, "Why not just interpret the dream?" Of course, you can do that, but by repeating it in an imagery, the client is back in the situation and can greatly expand on the story by your asking questions and interacting with the various characters in the dream.

For instance, a dream concerned an interaction with the client's parents, and something was said that was perceived as hurtful. Going back to that scene in an imagery could be an opportunity for the person who was hurt to express their feelings with the intention of working it out. The fun part of any imagery is that the client can in turn 'become' any of the characters. If the father was the one who was hurt by the mother, the client could be father and tell mother why he was hurt and then 'become' mother and respond.

Often, in an imagery we will suggest that the client ask the mother, for example, why she said what she said and the answer could be, "I have no idea what she would say?" Then we may ask if the client could 'become' the mother and they invariably say yes. Suddenly the answer to the question comes readily. That is one of the many miracles of imagery. Information comes that is usually accurate to the situation, even when the client isn't consciously aware of it. Either in an imagery experience or in just conversation, one of our favorite questions we ask clients when they are struggling with an answer to something is "If you did know the answer, what would it be?" You'd be amazed at some of the responses. Indeed, we know more than we think we know.

Another aspect of using a dream would be a nightmare, where the client suddenly woke up to avoid a terrible or threatening situation, and perhaps is still in an anxious state even several days later. It is best to start the imagery at the beginning of the dream, before the threat, and then continue to the place where they woke up. The difference is that in doing the imagery, the client starts in a relaxed place and they have the power and support of a therapist they trust. When approaching the actual threat in the dream, the therapist can suggest to the client that they 'freeze the frame', giving power and control of the situation to the client.

Then, the client and therapist can discuss the scene, the threat and the client's fear, while the scene is frozen and unable to continue. Even asking a bad guy, for example, "Why do you want to kill my client?" can start an amazing dialogue. It's surprising how often and how easily great information comes out, clarifies the emotions involved on both sides, creates ways of resolution or at least, brings new understanding.

SUB-PERSONALITIES

All of us have many sub-personalities or parts of us that can take over from time to time. Emotions can define us, including anger, fear, depression, anxiety, or even hope, curiosity, helpfulness and happiness. Roles can also define us, such as our occupation: teacher, lawyer, chef, or relational, such as being a husband, a wife, a son, a daughter, mother or father. Attitude and behavioral are also parts of us: the rebel, the coward, the aggressor, the victim, the oppressor. We're a plethora of roles and sub-personalities, some acting out appropriately while others not so appropriately. Emotions and sub-personalities can take over in an instant.

There are several ways to invite sub-personalities to appear in an imagery. We often use the setting of a meadow, invite the client to sit in a comfortable place and see a large boulder a few feet away. We continue to set the stage and might say, "Behind that boulder is a sub-personality that we need to talk to today. Ask it to come out from behind the rock and reveal itself to you. This sub-personality can come in any form it desires. What do you see? Ask the creature which part of you it represents."

Another great starting point is the use of animals. For example, if your client is dealing with anger issues, start the imagery with, "If your anger were an animal, what would it be?" Let's do a quick imagery and try that now.

QUICK IMAGERY
ANIMAL THAT REPRESENTS YOUR ANGER

Take a moment and just see your anger as an animal. Go with the first animal that pops up in your head.

What animal do you see? Describe it to yourself in great detail as to size, shape, color.

Where is the animal?

What is it doing?

Can you describe the personality of this animal?

The animal sees you for the first time. How does it react?

Can you become the animal? How do you feel as the animal?

As the animal, what are you the angriest about right now?

Look back at yourself, the person. How do you feel about this person?

Make a statement to the person about these feelings.

Become yourself again.

Stop and really reflect on what you saw and felt with our suggestions above. How do you feel about what just happened between you and this animal? What did you learn about the angry part of you? In person, we could talk about your anger for a long time and not learn as much as we could from that little exercise. Seeing your anger as an animal provides a certain distance and detachment from the general person you are. You have angry feelings, but you are not your anger, or your fear or any other emotional reaction, for that matter.

You are a person with varying emotions. By having your anger appear as an animal, it comes in pure form. No other conflicting emotion has been invited. It serves as a separate entity with its own set of values and behaviors. What did the animal feel about you? Did it like you or perhaps see you as weak or inadequate, unable to use the animal to protect yourself in tough situations?

It really doesn't make any difference whether the animal liked you or not. There is no judgment here. Remember, only information. If it liked and admired you, it might be because you're a fighter who takes no attitude from anyone and wins all your fights, someone the world might judge as a bully. If it didn't like you, it might be because it sees you as a coward, who runs away from a fight and can't protect yourself or your family. The animal can judge you good or bad all it wants. We don't want you to judge the information you received as good or bad; it's just information you can use for clarity and new understanding about yourself and why you behave the way you do.

INDIVIDUAL PEOPLE AS ANIMALS

The use of animals to symbolize any person or situation relevant to a client provides an easy and quick way of doing any imagery. The possibilities are endless: a parent, a boss, that final exam, your marriage, your future, any situation that could be upsetting you. Seeing a person, or pain, or problem as an animal is also an example of the way dreams communicate in our sleep. It's a method of seeing the person with fresh eyes, uncontaminated by guilt or known perceptions from the conscious mind. This allows the subconscious, where our emotions primarily function, to give us new information we might not normally understand or acknowledge.

One client saw her father as a huge, black bear. The best thing she liked about the bear was it was so big and strong and she knew that he could and would always protect her from the outside world. What she liked least was that when he was drinking, which was often, his anger was mostly expressed as physical and emotional abuse towards her. You might ask, "Hey, bears don't drink!" But, she is describing her father, who happens to be a bear and in an imagery, bears can drink. That's part of the magic of imagery and using symbols to represent people. The bear was her father in that moment, the total protector from the outside world and also, the drunk who abused her. When she saw her drunken father coming after her, he looked and felt like an enormous bear, angry, irresponsible and out of control.

She described him after the imagery as the person who gave her the most love and also inflicted the most pain. Those conflicting emotions and insights don't come up as easily in regular talk therapy. Here they were instant reactions and awareness. So whether we are dealing with our own sub-personalities or those of others, the purpose is the same; to learn from them, seek to understand their attitudes and issues and finally make peace with them.

Sometimes in dealing with childhood molestation or abuse, we have suggested the 'adult you' step into the room and speak to the perpetrator and say all the things they've never had the freedom to say to this person. Tell them how you feel and then defend and protect the 'child you'. This can be an empowerment the person has never felt before. Even if the child argued with, yelled at, or in some manner, confronted the father or person that molested them, most of the time the person did not react well in the real world; perhaps even denying it ever happened, blaming the child for seducing him or just getting mad. In the imagery, if the adult is asked to come and defend the child and tell the molester how they feel about him and what he did, many things can happen.

However, in experiencing their wounded child in an imagery, some clients, even when invited to bring in the strong, 'adult you' into the scene, cannot confront the parent or abuser, no matter how much protection you have afforded them. Keep asking questions, such as, "What are you feeling right now?" or "What is your fear of confronting this person?"

One client wanted to work on his relationship with his father. The client was in his seventies and the father had passed away many years before, but the hatred for the father, who had ridiculed and seemingly despised this little boy, was still intense. In an imagery, the father came as a vicious and fire-breathing dragon. The client could tell me in detail all the abuses as though they were yesterday, but could not say this to the overpowering figure before him.

He literally became the five year old in voice and body language, and could not become the adult man. The fear of the child overwhelmed the adult, who cringed in the situation. He kept saying he wanted to kill this awful beast, but could not speak the words to the dragon. Obviously the father had been dead for years. There was no relationship to lose. There were no consequences to be concerned with, but none the less, the client couldn't risk it. We offered the option to kill the bad dragon, 'bad father', so the client could then relate to the 'good father' who would remain. In imagery, any expression of violence either by the client or to the client is still just an imagery. If either one dies, the imagery will still go on, asking questions such as, "How does it feel to have killed the dragon or to be killed by the dragon?" and perhaps ask, "What do they have to say to each other?"

Finally, we invited the five year old to just tell the dragon how frightened and overwhelmed he felt. The client began to weep and sob, saying, "All I ever wanted was your love and approval. Look at me. I'm only five years old. How could you ridicule me like that? You have no idea how much I love you and need you. I love you." His hate had buried the child's love and need for his father. The client was shocked by his own words. The dragon became much smaller and gently cradled the little boy in his arms, saying, "I'm so sorry for what I did to you, your tiny body and overwhelming fear of life frightened me. I just wanted you to grow up to be a strong man like me. I am so sorry. Please forgive me." Can you feel the change going on in this little five year old hearing those words?

Many times in an imagery, a perpetrator who is defensive and mean will break down, confess and take responsibility for what happened and even beg forgiveness for the first time. It's as though the client got in touch with the real, scared and vulnerable part of the person that could never be revealed before. At this point, a healing can take place. It is much easier to forgive a repentant person who is truly sorry and takes full responsibility for his behavior. Accept the confession and apology, so they can release the trauma and stop the hatred that is hurting them today.

In quoting Martin Luther King, Jr., *He who is devoid of the power to forgive, is devoid of the power to love.* Forgiveness does not imply condoning hurtful or unacceptable behavior; but rather a releasing of the issue or trauma, choosing to not let it go on affecting one's life. To not forgive is to give total power over the rest of our life to the one who injured us. We become a victim, and we remain a victim just waiting for the perpetrator to say they're sorry.

If the molester denies or refuses to respond to the client's words of anger for what happened, we will often direct the client to step into the scene with the frightened child, before the rape or molestation, or whatever else the abuse contained; a child can be devastated by words and verbal abuse. Allow the client to pick up the child, love and comfort them, saying, "I'm so sorry you had to have this experience, but I am here now to protect you and love you." Then we would direct the client to turn to the perpetrator and say, "You have violated your right to parent this child. I'm removing them from this house, they will be my child now, and I will care for them." Now, still in the imagery, the client can take this child home to a new family, often bathing them, to symbolically clean off the past and putting them in a new bed for a soothing sleep.

When confronting any negative person, situation or animal, creating fear or anger, the 'freeze frame' is your best tool to stop the action, giving the client time to settle down, asking perhaps, "What are you feeling?" or "What would you like to do now?" Also, you can suggest additional protection, such as a glass partition between the client and the trauma or person. No one can get by that partition to hurt them. You can also offer a bodyguard to come into the scene to protect them.

In our certification program, which includes three separate weekend seminars, at least once during a weekend, we will demonstrate the one-on-one imagery technique with a volunteer. One particular student wanted to work on letting go of the rage she felt for her brother, who had molested her as a child. In the imagery, she was invited to see her brother walking towards her. She was so filled with anger, rage and fear, but she couldn't confront or utter a word. She was offered the fortification of a glass partition to protect her from her brother, but that didn't seem to comfort her, explaining, "He's clever. He can figure a way around it. He's coming to get me!" So, reaching for another tool, we suggested that she invite someone to come and help protect and defend her. She immediately saw her mother, and contrary to the expectation that mother came to calm her down, the client's anxiety immediately escalated, rather than subsided.

Then the rage came as she screamed, "Where were you to protect me? You didn't love me, I was just a kid. You didn't care!" The client was asked, "How is your mother responding to your words and what would she like to say to you right now?" And through the client's sobs, mother said, "I'm so sorry. I didn't believe you. You were both my children, I didn't know what to do. Can you ever forgive me?" In the discussion after the imagery, the client admitted that she didn't have a very close relationship with her mother and really couldn't figure out why. She gained some new truth; a new perspective.

In Marianne Williamson's words, *The places in our personality where we tend to deviate from love are not our faults, but our wounds. God doesn't want to punish us, but to heal us. And that is how He wishes us to view the errors in other people: as their woundedness, not their guilt.*

RELIVE A REAL INCIDENT OR TRAUMA

This starting point can be controversial. There are those who believe going back into an original trauma can trigger flashbacks and breakdowns, both physically and emotionally, especially with post-traumatic stress situations, often making things worse.

We believe there can be great healing in going back to the original source, but it is wise to use methods of protecting the client from the trauma itself. The 'freeze frame' is a potent and instant way to give the client control over any situation. We have never had a client who didn't react instantly to freezing the frame and stopping the action that was threatening them. In that moment, they have a control they never experienced in the real situation. Once the scene is frozen, the client is asked to just stay in that place. In a few seconds they are fairly calm and feel safe. Then we can talk about what they are seeing, what was about to happen next, and talk about the incident without going there.

As mentioned previously, other protections might be to suggest there is a glass partition between the client and the trauma and no one can get by that partition to hurt them. We can offer a bodyguard to protect them. In a childhood trauma, sometimes we have suggested the 'adult you' either step into the room or speak to the person or persons from behind the safety of the partition and say all the things they have never had the freedom or courage to say before; tell them how they feel and defend and protect the 'child you' that had no adult to protect them years ago. You can also suggest the client see a movie of the trauma, watching, but not experiencing, the trauma that the child was feeling.

One of our colleagues, Dr. Charlotte Reznick, authored an incredible book about using guided imagery with children, *The Power of Your Child's Imagination*. Before an imagery, she often suggests kids imagine a TV remote to hold, pointing out that they control the pause button. If something gets too scary, they have the power to stop the action or change the channel. What a beautiful gift of empowerment.

Years ago, we had a client wanting help in overcoming her fear of flying. Since imagery can be a marvelous tool in working with phobias, we figured easy enough. However, in hearing her story, we found out five years earlier she and her husband were part of just a handful of survivors of a horrific plane crash. On take-off, the plane struck some construction poles at the end of the runway, and burst into flames and crashed. This was not a phobia, but a real past trauma. She was planning her first flight since the accident the very next day, and as the time was rapidly approaching, her anxiety was unbearable. Knowing a little about imagery, she felt this was her only hope in getting through this all-consuming fear and giving her the courage to get on the plane.

In doing an imagery, we explained to her that she would always have the power to stop whatever started to unfold in the imagery and that in our dialogue during the experience, she would have control to 'freeze the frame' whenever it was necessary. This comforted her. And so we began, armed with all the tools that we could possibly need, including a protector, the glass partition and even the 'freeze frame' concept. Our starting point was inviting her to watch the scene, like watching a movie, being detached, seeing herself getting on the plane, getting settled in her seat, and starting the take-off. Her anxiety was mounting when she said that this was the last moment she could remember before the crash. We immediately said, "Freeze the frame right there. You're safe and nothing has happened yet."

In our conversation before the imagery she said she definitely believed in angels, so at this point in the imagery we invited her to see a beautiful angel appear, the angel that had protected her. She indeed saw a breathtaking vision and she started to cry. We asked her what was happening and through her tears she replied,

"I'm looking all around the plane, at all the passengers and they all have angels in front of them, caressing them, loving them." She described the scene with such detail, as if some of the angels were flying out of the plane with people, some of the angels were gently holding people and protecting them. We asked her what her angel was doing. She said that there were two angels, one was holding her hand and one was holding her husband's hand. She continued and said that these angels were inviting them to stand up and gently guiding them out of the plane. At this point, we were all in tears but we managed to ask her if there was anything she wanted to say to her angel and she just said, "Thank you."

Then we invited the angel to speak, "What would this angel like to say to you?" The angel said she would always protect her and keep her safe. At this point in the imagery, she and her husband were standing on the runway, the plane surrounded in white light with angels everywhere. The experience seemed complete and we ended by having the angel press the client's thumb and two fingers together, saying whenever she did this gesture, it would bring her back to this place of safety, protection and in the presence of her angel.

After the imagery, we told her that whenever she pressed her thumb and two fingers together, she would return to this place of miracles, of angels, of safety. Did she take the flight the next day? Indeed. Was she nervous? Of course, but her anxiety was manageable. We certainly can't change what happened to her, but she can unplug from the emotions wrapped around the actual event. That memory for her will always be there, but now the fear can be removed. Since the brain cannot distinguish between what's real and what's imagined, we do have the power to re-frame the trauma.

As mentioned in a previous chapter, Belleruth Naparstek's work with post-traumatic stress syndrome has earned her world renown and gained a new respect for the process of imagery to heal. In her book, *Invisible Heroes, Survivors of Trauma and How They Heal,* Belleruth often describes what she calls spontaneous imageries, where the client is in a crisis situation while in an imagery and is simply asked, "What would you like to do now?"

TAPPING INTO PERSONAL OR UNIVERSAL TRUTH

Many people are looking for concrete answers to help them with decision-making and planning for or understanding the future. Probably the majority of us don't trust our own inner wisdom. Either we are afraid we can't contact that true inner self or we just can't trust our own judgment, since we've made so many mistakes in the past.

We believe that 'prayer' is our method of contacting this universal truth, God, this higher power, asking for what we want, seeking guidance and direction, also to express gratitude. But when it comes to answers, it is extremely difficult to feel and trust that type of connection. Guided imagery can be a way to open the lines of communication. If you believe in God and/or the Universe, or a higher power, if you believe there is a plan for the earth and for us as individuals, then you must be a part of that plan and purpose.

Science tells us that every cell in our body is a microcosm of the entire body and our body is a microcosm of the entire universe. Gregg Braden, in his book, *The God Code,* explains, *By replacing the elements of DNA with their equivalent of Hebrew letters, we reveal the message that is spelled out within each cell of our bodies. By substituting these words for our genetic codes, we are now able to illustrate how the literal name of God forms the message within each cell of our bodies: God/Eternal within the body.* If all this is true, then we have a direct connection to all that is.

One of our favorite imageries, especially for those who have a strong personal faith, is to have the client experience just sitting in the lap of God or their higher power. Ask the questions they need to ask and listen for the answers. Let us pause here to say this is an absolute given in guided imagery; that you can see and talk to anyone or anything in an imagery state and get real answers: a God figure, a person, a tree, a symbol, a pain, it doesn't matter. As DeSoille so simply states, *In a dream or imagery, anything can happen.* And so, God, this higher power, can and will speak to us. Is this a message directly from God? Is it from a deep, higher connection with God-like truth? Is it from the highest source of our own essence and integrity, who knows what's best for us? To answer those questions, we'll leave that up to you.

Years ago, we had a male client, whose father had died several years before. There was a deep sense of sadness and even anger that there was a lot of unfinished business between them, and he couldn't let go of the frustration that it was now too late. We suggested doing do an imagery and talking to dad. He agreed, and we had a wonderful session. He saw himself sitting in the family living room where he asked questions, received answers, expressed his pain and anger and totally reconciled with his father. When he came out of the relaxed state of imagery, he was very pleased by what happened, but somewhat perplexed, asking, "What just happened? Was this a séance, was my dad actually here?" We laughed and said we didn't know. All we could tell him was that it happens often in imagery. Is it real? Is it just your imagination? Does it matter?

The next week he wanted to do a session with his mother, who was alive and lived about 20 miles away. He had the exact same experience of working things out with her in a way he didn't feel could have ever happened in person. When we finished, we asked him the questions, "What just happened? Was it a séance, was your mother actually here?" He laughed and we all agreed it didn't matter. He made peace with both his parents.

There are many symbols of wisdom and understanding we can use in an imagery to get our answers:

- A wise old man or woman – We usually end our weekend seminars with what we call a 'transformational imagery', to wrap up the seminar experience, to put all the pieces together and provide new wisdom and understanding. We often have the participants meet a wise old person and ask for direction, asking, "What have I learned and where do I go from here?"
- An Indian counsel – Sitting around a campfire at night with this counsel can afford an opportunity to ask for help and direction.
- Power animals – Some people have already established a relationship with a specific animal guide with whom they've become familiar and seek support and guidance.

- Guardian angels and spirit guides – People who believe strongly in guardian angels and pray to them or the saints they believe in, have a deep reverence for their wisdom.

We never question the beliefs of our clients or impose our own. If you want to talk to Buddha or some other hero of your faith, or anything else pops up unexpectedly in an imagery, that's ok. We've had clients spontaneously go into what obviously is a past life experience. How is that different than having a dream about a time many years ago? All dreams and imageries are metaphors or parables that speak of truth. As long as we are getting truth, and we recognize truth when we hear it, that's all that matters. When some truth or information doesn't make sense or doesn't fit in this context, we can challenge it, just like we would in an awake state.

Finally, let's talk about the people who don't wish to get answers from others and want to find their own truth. We live by a belief, which we will cover in more detail in a later chapter; at the core of every person is goodness. Some people don't believe in this concept. They would challenge and say, because of their belief in original sin, at the core of every person is evil, which can't be trusted and must be forgiven only by God. And even after being forgiven, evil still functions in their lives.

The Bible talks about our being created in the image of God. If we believe that verse, then the truth is that God is always within us and the God part of us is alive and well, whether we contact it or not. A plaque above Carl Jung's doorway in Switzerland reads, *Bidden or Unbidden, God is Present*. Many people give Jung the credit for this quote, however, it is the Latin translation from the ancient wisdom of Desiderius Erasmus.

Language speaks fluently in phrases such as the essence of our true self, integrity, character and conscience. This is the part of us that helps us live a moral and appropriate life. Abraham Maslow, in his own words, once described, *The top 2 % people as seemingly knowing what for them was absolute truth and couldn't be swayed*. We believe there is absolute truth within all of us and it is possible to make contact with that highest transpersonal self. Just because we don't or can't live there consciously all the time, we can still learn to contact and live by the true values of that source of wisdom.

In imagery, we often refer to that part of us as the inner mind or the full potential self. We can invite that part of us to come as a symbol of its own choosing and talk to it in the same manner as we discussed prior in talking to God or a wise person. We point out a word of caution. In all of our experience, Jesus, God, or any of the other sources of wisdom, will never criticize the client. In over forty years of doing this work that has been without exception. If you remember, in the Bible, the only people Jesus criticized were the scribes and Pharisees, the religious people of his day, whom he called, *Whited sepulchers, beautiful on the outside, but inside full of rotting, dead men's bones*. To the sinners, those he was criticized for socializing with, he simply said, *Go and sin no more.* In our imageries there has been nothing but loving support and direction, as well as ultimate forgiveness.

Be careful when you ask a symbol to come that represents the inner mind or true self. You may not always get what you ask for. If the one who comes and says he represents the true self is angry, is critical and tells you what's wrong with the client, that is not the true self, but a sub-personality and you can treat it as such. The true self is always forgiving and helpful in improving this person, without being critical of character. If a true self doesn't come, perhaps your client is not far enough along in working through their issues to acknowledge the true self and is not ready to accept the changes that would be required.

The unconscious mind is a marvelous combination of wisdom, discovery, humor and rituals for healing. Giving the options of asking, "What would you like to do with this situation now?" or "How would you like to handle it?" or "How would you like to heal this pain?" can bring answers, solutions and healing that the therapist could never have imagined. And, it will be something that resonates and feels right for the client, because it comes from deep within them, their own truth, their own authenticity, their own conquest.

The best part of doing an imagery is when the client is dialoguing and sharing what's happening. The therapist's role is to follow the client and help with suggestions or questions along the way, providing tools to help on the journey. Whether it's providing the ability to stop the action, bringing in a protector or providing the safety for the client to confront their demons and dragons, or talking to the true self or inner mind within them, imagery can work miracles. And remember, since the brain doesn't know the difference between what's real and what's imagined, we can mend a broken spirit.

Welcome Home

A brave young lad
Ventured forth in the world
Finding life an adventure
He grew to be a man

He experienced it all
The good and the bad
Tempted by all the dragons around
He lived, he lost, he fell

Now life was far from grand
His world was filled with pain
Traveling farther and farther
Away form home he wandered

Then one day, one fateful day
With strength he found
From deep within
He decided to return

Finding at last his home
In shock he entered a place of hell
Demons and dragons filled his head
A terror beyond his years

Instead of running fast away
He faced the monsters one by one
In sheer fright he honored them
And slowly they disappeared

All but one had vanished
This demon that remained
Was the meanest, the ugliest
The worst of all the lot

Rather than retreating away from home
This man freed this beast in love
He stated to sing
And stood square at the feet of his fears

In the flash of an instant
The last demon was gone
And the man was free at last
'Welcome home' was filling his heart

SUGGESTED CHAPTER STUDY

- By now, you should have a good understanding of where to begin an imagery. Create a starting point for a client who comes to you wanting to work on the continual conflict they are having with their boss. Where would you begin and set the stage, and what tools would you use in the experience?

- In doing a series of different imagery experiences with a client, it can be powerful to establish a wise person or healer that can be called upon regularly. This affords the client the opportunity to continually re-visit and consult for wisdom and peace.

CHAPTER EIGHT

KEEPING THE IMAGERY MOVING WITHOUT CONTROLLING THE OUTCOME

In facilitating a guided imagery with a group of people, each individual is experiencing the imagery silently and obviously, there's no opportunity for immediate feedback until after the experience. Then the group is generally invited to write down what they saw in some detail, followed by group discussion and interpretation. Group imageries are generally more structured as to what experience you, the therapist, intends the group to have.

If you want them to have a peaceful or relaxing experience, describe what you want them to see in great detail, such as:

It's a perfect day.
You find yourself in a large and beautiful meadow.
Birds are singing.
Smell the flowers.
Feel the grass beneath your feet.
The sun is shining and there is a gentle breeze caressing your face.

The temperature of the air on your body is just right as it touches your skin.

If you wish for the group to have a more tentative or probative experience, you might set the stage with:

You find yourself in a dark cave, or in a shadowy place.
It's nightfall.
There are strange sounds.

These examples are a more structured approach. You are basically telling them what you want them to see, feel and experience in the moment. In a one-on-one imagery, after the induction, the client will be talking, thereby allowing the therapist to be more a part of the imagery experience, responding to the client's descriptions and following them on the journey.

Let's go back to the meadow motif:

You find yourself in a meadow.
Stand there for a moment and take it all in.
What size is your meadow?
Describe what you see in great detail.
What is the weather like?
What are the smells?
How do you feel just being there?

STRUCTURE VERSUS OPEN ENDED APPROACH

Suggesting various things to be aware of tends to anchor the client into a more personal imagery experience; unique to them. This is different than telling the client what to see. You can continue to gently guide by following the client, asking questions and responding to what they share.

For example, see an animal. A structured approach would be:

Is it large or small?

Male or female?
Friendly or angry?

An open ended approach would be:

What is your overall impression of this animal?
Describe the animal.
How does it relate to you?
What do like best?
What do you like least?
Become the animal.
What do you feel as the animal?

Can you see how, even in the group imagery, you can be more open in your questions and allow the clients to have their own spontaneous experiences? People don't always follow the therapist's direction or even want to, for that matter. By giving more open ended suggestions, you are providing more spontaneous reactions and experiences to unfold. Even telling people to see a horse will bring a varied reaction of multiple horses with individual personalities and responses.

Ok, so you've done the induction, you have a starting point, now how do you keep the imagery moving without controlling the outcome? Your desired outcome may be appropriate, but not the right one for the client. Always follow the client. Don't force the experience of where you want it to go or where you think it should go.

We were working with a client who had stomach cancer. He saw the tumor as a large octopus. In setting up the experience, we invited a healer to come, and together, the client and the healer, in no way harmful to the body, pulled this animal out of his stomach. We dialogued with the octopus.

We asked the animal our three classic questions and got some great information:

- What would you like to tell us?
- What do you need from the client that you're not getting?
- How would life be different if you got what you needed?

Can you see how the above questions could be used in a number of different imagery situations? At the end of the imagery, we asked him if he wanted to take the octopus back into his body where it came from or let it go free. It's important to ask that type of question without judgment, there's no right or wrong answer. Whatever the client does is appropriate and must be honored. He struggled for awhile and finally said, "I want to take it back inside where it belongs." Our first reaction was to say, "Are you sure?" But we held our tongues. Obviously, there was more information from the octopus, and in subsequent imageries we had an incredible journey with the creature.

After the imagery, the client shared his feelings in more detail about the octopus, and we read the meaning of octopus according to Ted Andrews in his book *Animal-Wise*, quoting the passage, *The octopus reminds us to not immerse ourselves so deeply in our tasks that we forget to take care of ourselves.* Being an overworked executive, he smiled and said, "I wish I had a dollar for every time I've said my job is going to kill me."

Suggestions to keep the imagery moving could include:

Tell me what you see.
Let anything happen.
How would you describe the personality of that symbol?
Go on.
Tell me more.
Talk about your fear, your anger, your pain, whatever.
What's it like to be controlled by this fear, this anger, this pain?
What would you like to do now?

Questions to ask the symbol could include:

What is your meaning or issue in my life?
What is the most important thing you want me to know about you?
About me?
About the problem?

What do you want from me you're not getting?
How would life be different if I gave you what you just asked for?
What would life be like without this pain?
What are the benefits of this pain?
Why haven't I changed this situation before?
What am I the most afraid of?
What blocks me from changing?
Ask for advice or direction.
If you could change the person in any way, what would you do?
Let anything happen that wants to happen?
Have a spontaneous experience.
What's happening now?
Tell me more.

You don't want to barrage the client with a million questions. Give the client time to process each question and allow them to respond. Use no more than three of these questions and link them together, one at a time, allowing sufficient time for feedback from the client.

HOW ABOUT THE UNEXPECTED

In talking to a sub-personality, a person in the client's life, a symbol of any kind, or an animal, you may find vicious anger towards the client with, perhaps the statement of, "I hate this person and I want to kill them!" Stop right there and be in that situation. As the therapist, you're talking to an animal that threatens to kill your client. Feel that. What is the first thing you want to say? What's your intent right now? Was your first reaction fear, anger at the animal, the need to protect your client? Perhaps you have no idea what to do.

There is no judgment here. Whatever you felt is just truth, information. Is it ok for the symbol to be angry enough to kill your client; to be demanding, critical, threatening? Yes, it is. Is your first thought to protect or correct or challenge back? Probably. In a real life situation, the need to protect yourself or your client is a natural reaction.

Dr. Carl Rogers, the psychologist known for his client centered therapy, developed the technique of feeding back to the client what was just said. The client would say, "I hate my mother." Rogers would say, "Oh, you hate your mother." Rogers often said he gave no advice or suggestions to clients and never wanted to be seen as an authority figure. Rogers tells the story of when he was confronted with a young man who insisted he was going to commit suicide. After a few tries of his usual approach with no success, he leaned over his desk and said to the young man, "I don't believe I am going to let you do that." Even the gentle, soft spoken Rogers came to a point where saving the client was a very real need and obligation.

However, imagery provides us with more latitude and options. It really doesn't matter what happens, it's only imagery. An angry symbol or animal might say, "I want to kill this person." An unfriendly message is wonderful. This is what we're looking for in any guided imagery experience; dealing with an internal conflict as not good or bad, just information.

Open Ended Answer might be:

That's interesting.
What has the client done that makes you mad enough to want to kill them?
Tell me more about your anger.

Be very aware of how the above questions responded to the threat. There was no reaction to the accusation. The questions actually honored the feelings of the symbol making the threat, "That's interesting, what has the client done that makes you mad enough to want to kill him?" The topic immediately changed from the act of killing, to the feelings of the angry person, "Tell me more about your anger."

If you listen and re-frame the situation from action to saying, "Tell me the reasons you feel this way," the symbol making the threat usually will calm down. His feelings of anger have been acknowledged as legitimate and real, and he is being listened to at last, someone heard his pain hiding beneath the angry threat. In spite of what we just said, the angry symbol may expect anger in return and a knee-jerk reaction might be defensive, with a comment like, "Who in the world are you?" How would you respond to that? A good answer could be, "Someone who comes in peace and wants to listen to you and learn from you. I feel you have a lot of helpful information." Remember, no judgment. Interestingly enough this might be the best approach in a real life situation, too. The best way to stop an argument is to stop arguing and listen.

So, continue the dialogue by honoring the symbol or animal:

I have a strong feeling you have good reason to be mad at this person.
You have much to offer if they would listen.
It sounds like you've tried to protect them from worse pain in their
    life.
You must be very frustrated that your advice and help is being ignored.
You're not getting your needs met either.
It sounds like you still see this person as a child and are angry at the
    decisions that were made when they were a child.
You are still treating this person as a child who needs child-like discipline.
This person is an adult now and has power and skills that were not
    present as a child.
Maybe we need a new approach.

Let's use another example. Earlier we put you in a room called anxiety with an adjoining room called calm. Let's change that. The issue is fear.

QUICK IMAGERY
A DOOR MARKED FEAR

You find yourself at the far end of a long corridor.

Directly in front of you is a huge door.

The name on the door is FEAR.

What are you feeling as you look at the door?

You know on the other side of that door is violent anger.

Be very aware of all the details of the door, size, color, door knob, thickness.

Someone behind you wants you to go through that door. What feelings come up?

Put your hand on the door, what do you feel? Touch the handle, is the door locked?

What do you feel would happen if you opened the door?

How would you feel to just walk away and never open that door?

Slowly, come back to this room.

If you actually did the imagery, we suggest you write down your experience. This is a test of values and expectations when experiencing a very fearful situation. How did you feel when told that someone behind you wants you to go through that door? Were you angry and rebellious at the thought of pressure from an authority figure telling you what to do? Did you feel obligated to obey because you were taught to do what others think is correct? Were you taught to go through every door and face your fears? If you walked away, would you feel like a coward? Could you walk away and feel good about yourself because you had no need to take unnecessary and perhaps foolish risks?

Remember, there's no judgment about your decision and why you made it. This is all to provide information about the way you perceive and respond to unpleasant choices. How much of your decision making is still tied to childhood training, and how much have you broken those ties and now act from your own values, beliefs and experience? Knowing where you are now is the first step towards understanding why you react the way you do, especially under stress, and how you might want to change.

HOW TO HANDLE PANIC AND ANXIETY IN THE IMAGERY

Have you ever been with a child in the middle of a nightmare, perhaps thrashing around in the bed, making strange noises? The last thing you want to do is shake them awake and say, "Wake up. You're having a bad dream." If you do that, they may bring the dream emotions back with them in that forced awake state.

What is preferred is to gently rub their arm or back and whisper, "I'm right here. Everything is fine. I'm here. I'll help you." Within seconds they will wake up, see you there and perhaps say, "Oh, hi!" and be comforted.

If you touch them firmly or grab them, they could incorporate you into the dream and experience you as the bad guy they were afraid of. The same principle applies even stronger in imagery. If your client is suddenly in a panic from something happening or about to happen in the imagery, perhaps a flash back to a real life situation, the best thing you can do, as we've mentioned before, is a gentle statement of 'freeze the frame'.

We've never had a client who didn't respond to that statement. You will note that in a few seconds, the client's body will begin to relax. You could ask then what they are feeling now. Usually that question is answered with, "I'm calmer now. Everything has stopped." Now you can talk about the scene and why it was so frightening. What you did with this brief command was give all the power to the client, possibly for the first time in their life. The client can feel in total control. The action was stopped dead in its tracks. Now you can ask the client, "How do you wish to proceed?" With the power given to them, they might choose to continue the scene and see what happens. Another option you can offer is to suggest that the client remove the conscious self from the scene and watch from a distance.

PATTI: When I was 17 years old, I lost my parents in a car accident. As we will discuss in more detail in the next chapter about belief systems, you can only imagine the beliefs that were instilled in that moment about myself, about my world. Adding to the devastating grief of their loss, and because they were driving down to visit me at college, I felt an additional, overwhelming sense of guilt. It was my fault.

In her book, *Molecules of Emotion*, Dr. Candace Pert has discovered that all authentic emotions are healing. Rather than denying or repressing these feelings, the expression of each and every emotion can send a host of positive chemicals throughout the body. Her research has shown that with every spontaneous remission, the event was preceded by a strong episode of anger or rage. There is one exception to this full range of healing emotions, and that is guilt and shame. The expression, being poisoned by guilt, takes on a whole new meaning, doesn't it?

Going back to the trauma of my parents' death, through a guided imagery, I was able to watch the events of the accident, like watching a movie. Of course, I was not in the car when the accident happened, but my imagination created the scene, with me in the back seat of the car, watching us drive down the highway. My anxiety was building and right before the crash, I was instructed to 'freeze the frame'. That felt so empowering. I was able to talk with my mother, sharing with her my feelings, and she told me that she loved me and would always watch over me. To this day, I believe her.

I was able to talk with my father, sharing my feelings of love, and he assured me the accident was not my fault. Since we keep repeating that everything experienced by the brain is real, perhaps in that moment, my father's words wiped away over twenty years of guilt. We can't do anything about our history, our traumas, but we can change and unplug from the emotions wrapped around all those events. When asked in the imagery if I wanted to continue the scene and watch the accident, I choose not to proceed, but rather just watched as we all left the car. I chose not to go any further with the imagery. Was that ok? Of course.

There are many situations where freezing the frame can be a valuable tool. It could be the decision of the client, who wishes to not proceed into the panic of a past trauma, or the therapist, who wants to stop the action and dialogue with the client about their feelings in the moment. This happens often with abuse or molestation from a parent or family member. For example, a client approaches a room and suddenly panics, knowing the person they fear is in that room. Freezing the scene gives total control to the client. Within seconds you will note the client starts to relax and is in control of self and the situation.

You start by reassuring the client that this person is truly frozen in time and can't hurt them. If they need more protection you can suggest there is that glass barrier between them so they can see each other, but the perpetrator can't cross that space. You could even supply a body guard, if needed. Now you can tell the client that they have several choices, asking, "What would you like to say to this person who can no longer hurt you?" Many times the person, remember the client is experiencing all this as the child, will scream out in anger at the father, or whoever, with profanity and rage. At last, authentic feelings finally are given permission to be expressed.

CHUCK: Patti shares her journey with cancer and often relates the episode when she was at one of her medical review sessions. All her doctors were involved, sitting on one side of the table, with her alone on the other side. They began speaking about her, rather than to her, and she rapidly lost her identity and it was just about a brain tumor. When she told me about this, I immediately asked, "What did you do? What did you say?" She smiled and with such strength, told me she stood up, lifted up her side of the table, papers and coffee cups sliding off, and proclaimed in rage, "Never refer to me as my cancer! I'm a person, not a tumor!" The healing power of her rage, her truth! I wish I had been there. That was the beginning of her healing. Reiterating Dr. Pert's statement that, preceding every spontaneous remission she studied, there was an episode of anger or rage.

We must stop for a moment for an explanation. Some people would judge this reaction as inappropriate. Why would you allow your client to express that rage? All displays of anger are bad, right? Wrong. All authentic emotions are healthy, increase the immune system and are appropriate. To repress them over years and years due to guilt or fear can literally makes us ill. Anger is not good or bad. Anger is simply energy and feelings. Without anger, or being denied the expression of our rage, keeps us a vulnerable victim. One of our favorite books is *Feelings Buried Alive Never Die* by Karol K. Truman. The title says it all.

In an imagery experience, sometimes the client, experiencing molestation as a child, even with all the protection of a body guard, a partition, still can't express their anger. An option here could be to suggest that the 'adult you' enter the scene and pick up the child. Holding and loving the child, telling them how sad the 'adult you' is that the child had to go through these horrible experiences, and how proud they are that the child survived all this abuse. Then the 'adult you' is asked if there is anything they would like to say. Most of the time, the adult can, with or without anger, tell the perpetrator what a terrible thing they did to this innocent little child, and they need to apologize.

As you know, we cannot predict how the oppressor will respond. We have seen everything from tears and deep regret with warm and sincere apologies, to silence and withdrawal, or even denial that they ever hurt the child. Often, this is what happens in real life when a perpetrator is confronted. However, the chances of a positive response are often better in a guided imagery. It's as though the client has made contact with the true self of the aggressor, underneath the crust of anger and meanness. Regardless of the reaction or response, we usually suggest to the adult to take this little child out of the situation. Then the client can remove the child from the scene, take over the parenting role and meet this child's needs from now on.

What if neither the child nor the adult wishes to continue by confronting the perpetrator? That's ok. You don't criticize the client's decision. Making sure the client is relaxed, summarize what happened to that point, commenting on how brave they were, and that they had the power to protect the child and did it well. Now end the imagery by slowly bringing the client back to the room.

In Belleruth Naparstek's work with post-traumatic stress victims, one of her techniques in imagery is to invite the client to imagine what they would like to see happen, changing the event. Of course, we can't change the history. However, we can change our perceptions. Referencing the imagery with the survivor of the plane crash in Chapter Seven, we can't change history; that hundreds of people horrifically died. But, we can re-frame their death as being caressed in the arms of angels flying up to heaven.

CHUCK: I'd like to close this chapter with a beautiful example of the power of the unconscious and the imagery experience. A young woman, perhaps in her late thirties came to deal with the molestation she experienced by her father. She left home in her late teens and had not seen or had any contact with him since. In an imagery, she had her father come into the room. She told him she needed to tell him how angry and incomplete she felt with him and wanted to express all the ways he hurt her and violated her. He simply replied that he understood and would listen, something he'd never done in real life. She spent some time going over the sordid details and how angry she was. By the time she finished, he was a broken man, in tears.

He profusely confessed that she was correct and none of it was her fault. He begged her to forgive him. She broke into tears, saying, "Daddy, thank you for admitting your guilt and asking for forgiveness. Of course, I will forgive you. Now I can have a relationship with you again." In the imagery, he stopped her at once, saying, "No, dear, don't call or contact me. I admitted to you that I did those things because I was a very sick man. But I haven't changed. I'm sorry I did that to you, but if you came to me today, as the beautiful woman you are, I'd do it again. I can't control myself. Just know that I'm so sorry for what I did and who I am. And thank you for forgiving me."

Where did that information come from? Was he really there in the room? Is this from her subconscious? I don't know. I do believe that deep in our subconscious resides all of our truth and that on some level we are all connected. Call it her integrity, insight, wisdom from the Universe, whatever you wish. We often say, "Prayer is when we talk to God. Imagery is a way for God to answer."

We conclude this discussion with a word about 'false memory syndrome'. In the early 1990's, there was a great controversy about whether past memories about molestation and other abuse uncovered in hypnosis or therapy were actually real events or contrived through suggestion or coercion from the therapist. We have mentioned many times that everything experienced in the brain, actual life events and imaginary episodes, is experienced as real. It is easy to see how false memory syndrome could exit.

An example, Becky, a nine year old girl, spends the night with her girl friend. During the night, the friend tells Becky that her father has been molesting her for a number of years and goes into graphic detail about what happens. Becky had no knowledge of this type of behavior. It is almost a given that Becky will have dreams that night of being molested by her father.

Whenever a child hears about anything new like this, especially something shocking and vivid, the child will dream about having a similar experience. What would it feel like to have this experience? All children use their imaginations and dreams to project what older people are doing. Its part of growing up; acting out the behavior in the safety of their own fantasies. Twenty years later, Becky is in therapy for other reasons and has a guided imagery or hypnosis experience and sees herself being molested by her father. What she is actually remembering is her very vivid childhood dream.

We have done many imageries with clients where a situation, very graphic and clear, spontaneously came up that they were being molested by some member in their family. One lady actually saw her father and his male friend having a fist fight because the friend wanted to participate, too. When she was brought out of the imagery, the first question is, "Did that really happen? I have no conscious memory of that." When the imagery is vivid and feels so traumatic, it is sometimes difficult for the therapist to avoid saying, "Yes, I believe it happened." Our answer, however, is always the same, "We don't know." If the client has no memory of it in real life and the relationship with their parents is ok today, let's assume it did not happen.

But, the fear is real. Perhaps you were constantly told as a child growing up that all men were obsessed with sex and wanted to molest you. Don't trust any man. Or you could have been told by a friend or heard in school about someone being raped. All these could account for the experience in the imagery. It's the fear that obviously needs to be explored further. We can address this by doing the imagery again and change the experience by freezing the frame, helping the child confront the offender and send him away. Or perhaps, have the adult come in and defend the child. Then, remove the child with the suggestion that when they leave this room they will leave the trauma behind so that it will never affect them again. The same approach as if it really did happen.

SUGGESTED CHAPTER STUDY

- Understand the difference between the structured and open ended approach in asking questions during an imagery. Always give the client the freedom to unfold the experience in their own way.

- In doing the quick imagery, 'A Door Marked Fear', did you learn anything new about yourself?

- When encountering any traumatic situation in imagery, remember the 'freeze frame'. This gives the client the sense of power to stop any situation, and also affords you, the therapist, the opportunity to take a breath and think about how to proceed.

CHAPTER NINE

A WORD ABOUT BELIEF SYSTEMS

A client came to us wanting to work on his anxiety. He was continually feeling unsettled, unsafe and anxious all the time. Even taking pharmaceuticals, such as Prozac or Paxil, didn't seem to quiet his apprehensions. Looking back at some of his relationships, he could see a pattern of sabotage and mistrust with everyone. You could start an imagery, of course, with "Where in your body to you feel this anxiety?" or even, "See an animal that represents these anxious feelings." Good places to begin, however, but let's look at another approach.

According to John Bradshaw, the renowned psychologist who introduced the concept of the wounded child in the 1970's, approximately 80% of all our values, virtues and beliefs about self are developed by the time we are six or seven years old. That young mind really doesn't have the tools to intellectually sort out information as right or wrong, real or unreal. And further, since we are told that children are ego centered, all situations and events they experience are judged positively or negatively about them. If mommy and daddy are arguing, it's the child's fault. If mommy tells them to go away, they don't have the maturity to perhaps conclude that she has a headache and wants to be alone for awhile. In their self-absorbed processing, in that moment a belief system could be established that, "I'm not loveable. I'm not worthy."

In our formative years, all these events do shape us and how we perceive and feel about ourselves. They can be negative and devastating, "Why can't you be more like your brother?" or, "You'll never amount to anything!" Or, they can be empowering. They all get thrown in that 95% of our subconscious, which truly rules our behavior.

As quoted in *Spontaneous Evolution*, by Bruce Lipton, *Our subconscious is running the show 95% of the time. Therefore, our fate is actually under the control of recorded programs or habits, that have been derived from instincts and the perceptions acquired in our life experience. The most powerful and influential programs in the subconscious mind are the ones that were recorded first. During the extremely important formative period between gestation and six years of age, our fundamental life-shaping programs were acquired by observing and listening to our primary teachers – our parents, siblings, and local community.*

It's curious that Freud felt the subconscious mind represented 90%, with the remaining 10% divided equally between the conscious and the preconscious. In his psychoanalytic theory, this preconscious mind included memories which were not conscious, but could be retrieved into our awareness at any time. Think about some of the events from your childhood, some of the statements made to you from parents or teachers. Think about some of the traumatic moments from your past and what beliefs that child established. A teacher saying, "You are so stupid", could become a self-fulfilling prophesy.

In a previous chapter, we talked about a woman who, in an imagery, saw her father as a bear. She shared that dad had molested her. In further exploring the imagery, we discovered her inability to be close with her mother, who apparently had been a good parent. However, think again about the belief formulated during the molestation. Perhaps she would say, "Mom doesn't care. She wasn't there to protect me." All subconscious, these beliefs are alive and well in our behavior and attitudes.

Now, let's go back to our client with anxiety. Listening to his story, his history, we learned his mother gave him up at birth and he was not adopted until six month of age. Even at such a young age, that infant experienced feelings of abandonment and unworthiness, formulating a belief of, "I'm not good enough. There's nobody to protect me. Nobody wants me." We further learned that at around age nine, he severely injured his hand and he actually verbalized his anger at his mom, screaming, "Where were you to protect me?" His teen years brought an adventure of drug use, and at age sixteen, he was arrested. His adopted parents, in an attempt to provide a tough love approach, allowed him to spend the night in jail. Again, what belief systems were established and re-enforced? Whether they were true, accurate or appropriate to the situation, the ugly head of the original statement of, "There's nobody to protect me," became his mantra.

In adulthood, with these belief systems of unworthiness and abandonment still an active part of his unconscious, he could see how he sabotaged all his relationships. Remember, this vast 95% of subconscious information has no judgment of good or bad, right or wrong. It just is, and that's the way it's supposed to be. So, if a relationship started to develop that would show his worthiness or offer support, he would desperately do or say something to prove or reinforce his original belief of unworthiness; something that would sabotage and drive them away. He might say, "See, I told you, I'm not good enough. There's nobody to protect or support me." A self-fulfilling prophesy; all beyond our conscious awareness.

So, a starting point in this type of approach to guided imagery would be to visit that infant. Even though a six-month infant is pre-verbal and unable to speak, through imagery, inviting the client to 'become' the baby, invariably brings an incredible dialogue. The following is part of the journey:

We invite you to see that little you, just a few months old. Do you see him?
Yes.

What do you feel just looking at him?
He's so little and perfect. He seems so alone.

Can you become this infant?
Yes.

What are you feeling as this infant?
I feel so alone, I feel so abandoned. There's no one here to protect me. I feel lost. I'm scared.

What are you scared of?
I'm scared of being alone.

Where is your mother?
I must not be worth much since my mother won't even be with me. She's supposed to be here to protect me.

We understand. That must be scary. But, there's someone here right now who wants to meet you. Do you see that man standing there?
Yes, who is that?

It's you in about thirty years. Would you like to meet him?
Yes.

At this point, still in the imagery, the client is asked to become himself again and look back at the child.
What would you like to say to this child?
I'm so sorry you have to go through this. It wasn't that your mother didn't love you. It had nothing to do with you. She just wasn't able to care for you. I want to love you.

The dialogue between them went on for quite awhile, and we asked what he would like to do with the child, and immediately he responded with, "I want to take this baby home with me." Perhaps with just this one experience, we were able to re-frame that belief system from "I'm not worthy," to "I am worthy and loveable." Changing "There's nobody to protect or support me" to "I will always be safe and I will always find support." Since the brain cannot distinguish between what's real and what's imagined, we truly believe a healing occurred.

Also, according to the latest theory of quantum physics, and the findings of Dr. Fred Alan Wolf, there is no concept of time and all things, past and future, are happening simultaneously. If this is true, on some level, that little baby felt a surge of love and protection during the imagery. If you are having difficulty with the idea that all things are happening in this moment, consider this. Astronomers are developing new and better telescopes that can look deeper and deeper into the heavens, finding new galaxies; new black holes they didn't know existed before. They are literally going deeper and deeper into time and say they are very close to seeing the big bang itself; the origin of our universe. If we can see and witness these events in the sky from millions of years ago, then they still exist. Even stars that burned out millions of year ago are still seen today.

PATTI: All my life, I have been claustrophobic. I remember as a child, feeling uncomfortable in tight, small places. A blanket over my head drove me wild. As an adult, I never liked closed doors, always opening curtains, drapes or blinds upon entering a room. Going through the diagnosis of cancer, the MRI and CT scans always created extreme anxiety for me. Lying still during radiation with restrictive head clamps wasn't possible without heavy sedation. My phobia seemed to be getting stronger and stronger, driving me into sheer panic the night before any type of procedure.

I tried to remember my past, some incident from my early childhood that could have triggered this exaggerated feeling. I couldn't recall anything, and then one day, Chuck suggested we try imagery. Through the process, this could allow my mind to review my childhood, unlock a possible forgotten memory of being scared or frightened. This event could still be held with all the associated emotions, as a muscle memory, unconsciously triggering my anxiety and claustrophobia now.

In the relaxed place of imagery, Chuck suggested that I see myself as a child, feeling scared, fearful and asked, "What's happening? What's going on?"

I see me at nine years old, feeling extremely paranoid about being in my bedroom with the door closed. Nothing threatening but she is feeling very claustrophobic.

Now, go back to an earlier time when she first experienced these feelings.

I see me at about three years old, scared and frightened.

All of a sudden, it was like watching a movie, I saw this little girl. I was asleep in the back seat of my parents' car. I could see my mom and dad helping my grandmother out of the car, watching them assist her into the house. Then, this little me woke up, alone, frightened, abandoned, wondering where everyone was. I watched myself start to cry, struggling to get out of the car, in a dark, closed garage. The child was screaming in total panic as she slipped out of the car, hit her head on the floor, unconscious now, blood everywhere. Within moments, I see both my parents run out to the garage, hearing my screams. In their concern of getting grandma settled in the house, each of them thought the other had already carried me safely into the house.

This three year old felt such panic of abandonment, confusion and fear. The struggle to get out of the car, along with the head injury, created a muscle memory. Triggered when in closed places, would bring back all the same terror. What was the belief system instilled in that moment? At this point, Chuck asked me to go back and see the little girl when she first wakes up, before she begins to panic. He told me to see the 'adult you' climb into the car and keep the child company until my parents return. See the child safely being carried into the house in the strong arms of daddy.

Obviously, if this was an actual event from my past, an experience I had no memory of in my conscious mind, no amount of changing the sequence of events in an imagery, often referred to as re-framing, can alter the history of what really happened to me. However, by isolating the actual event in my mind, bringing it from the unconscious to the conscious level, I can then separate the emotional trauma from the actual memory of the experience. The event will always be there, it happened, but the emotional response or belief systems created can be changed, thus removing the feelings of panic and fear.

I have no memory of this experience, and I have no way of asking my family what really happened. All three people in my imagery, my mom, dad and grandmother are dead, however, with a hand mirror I found a small scar on the back of my head. Did it really happen? I don't know for sure, but a frightened child was comforted. After the imagery, my anxiety seemed to slowly disappear. Whenever I had to endure an MRI or similar procedure, I found myself comforting and loving that precious little girl. My claustrophobia seemed to fade the more I visited and honored this child.

Similarly, we can't change the history of our client and the mother who gave him up for adoption, but we can give that infant comfort and safety. Through the process of imagery, we can travel back in time to provide support, thus changing that little one's belief about the world being scary and his being unworthy. Traveling back in time is simply taking the client back to revisit a trauma that greatly affected them as a child. An example could be a boy of nine years old in a school room, asking the teacher to go to the bathroom and her responding with annoyance or irritation and refusing to let him leave the room. He wets his pants a few minutes later and is then made fun of by the teacher, and laughed at by the entire class.

We can stop the scene and have the adult client come into the room and speak to the teacher, sometimes with anger or often with the gentleness that the teacher never showed the child, and point out the inappropriate decision made to not allow the child to go to the bathroom, compounding the trauma by embarrassment and ridicule in front of his peers. In an imagery, the adult could then ask the teacher to apologize to the child and the class and admit she was wrong. Most of the time, this will happen. But even if the teacher still blames the child, the adult could take this issue to the principal and not stop until it was corrected, much like many parents have done in real life. That changes the child's feelings from being helpless against authority, to feeling supported and loved; from being a victim to being a winner.

What were the belief systems that shaped your life? Which of your parents defined you? Were you the pretty one or the smart one, the good child or the troublemaker, the black sheep or the athlete, having to live up to unrealistic expectations, or to put up with ridicule or physical abuse? Let instances of this come to your mind, right now. Stop for a moment and answer the questions about your identity and how it was forged, and is still affecting you today. Even positive statements, such as being the pretty one or the smart one, can have negative connotations to the child. Being pretty may make the child feel that they are not smart or if smart, then not pretty. The child needs to feel loved for who and what they are as a total being, not one favorable or unfavorable aspect. We define unconditional love as, "I love you because you exist and need no other reason to love you."

The job description of our parents is to teach us rules and regulations, morals and values, right from wrong, what is acceptable and not acceptable in our outside world. The job description of the child is to test those boundaries; to find out if the parents plan to enforce these values, asking, "How far can I go to push these boundaries before you stop me?" The child is really asking for limits, but is usually not aware of that. Can you see the making of some conflict here? Who has the power to win? Some of you parents reading this may respond, "The kids, of course!" Yes, there are some children who seem very determined to try and win. However the child is no match for the larger, stronger and powerful adults. The terrible two's and the terrible teens have a lot in common, however the teens have a better chance of winning the war, which is usually not good for anyone.

Another job description of the parents is to provide unconditional love to their children. But, how do you love the unlovable child, the child who seems to have come into this world angry and rebellious, hyper and mean-spirited? The way to do that is to separate the child from the behavior. There are those who don't believe this is possible and will argue that you are your behavior. Whatever you do or say identifies your character. But, children and sub-personalities act out, whether by rebellion or withdrawal, because they feel unloved. The message to the child needs to be, "I love you unconditionally and nothing you can do will stop me from loving you. But your behavior is unacceptable and I will do anything in my power to stop you from being destructive to yourself and others. My job is to protect you from yourself and teach you how to set your own limits."

Best selling author Carolyn Myss tells us that as teenagers grow up, they need to separate from their parents and find their own personhood. Going to school, learning from friends and society, they find that not everyone in the world shares the same values as their parents. There are political, religious and even moral beliefs that vary throughout society. So, as they grow up, they accept many or most of the values of parents, but perhaps strongly differ in others. Let's say their parents were extremely rigid in their particular religious beliefs. As the child gets older, he may not accept these values anymore and makes a conscious decision to reject them.

Or, the parents have a high regard for education and push the child to get a doctorate and be a professional. Perhaps the child feels inadequate to achieve those goals, or just wants to become a mechanic and have his own garage. He goes his own way, and feels very confident and secure in these decisions. Then crisis comes. Do you remember your first crisis in life? How devastating and overwhelming it seemed? Then, Myss tells us, the child who has become an adult, tends to revert back to their childhood beliefs, their childhood methods of coping. At this point, it is not the adult who is reacting to stress, but the small child. What did you do as a child in the face of stress? Did you curl up in fear and panic, lash out and be violent, withdraw from the situation, get ill or have an asthma attack?

In our work with imagery, we constantly stress that imagery provides instant access to the unconscious and that's where the real battles are occurring. Our job is to help you make peace with the false belief systems that control you. Imagery gives you the ability to bring these issues out of the dungeon of the unconscious up to the light of day, where they can be looked at, talked to and loved. The illustrations at the beginning of this chapter provided an example of that.

In our certification program we set aside two full days for the subject of healing and re-parenting the wounded child. Here is a brief outline of the goals of this work:

- Feel and experience the child's hurt. Don't deny that hurt or run away from it, or reject the child. It's ok to grieve and feel their pain. Understand the belief systems the child developed to cope with pain or disappointment.

- Understand what happened to the child and forgive the child for being helpless and weak.
- Forgive the aggressor for their sickness and behavior.
- Re-parent this child. Reclaim this child. Love this child, it's your child.

Unfinished issues from our childhood are the biggest handicap to our present and our future. Most of the time we keep these issues hidden from our everyday functioning, buried in the unconscious mind, so we can go about the business of life with minimal discomfort or even awareness. Our deep issues of the wounded child within, of insecurity, prior trauma, fear and the tendency to be a victim, don't seem to be an every day experience.

Then crisis comes, personal crisis, such as the loss of a job, impending divorce or illness, or a global crisis such as earthquakes, the economic recession, random shootings, or the thought of terrorism; all those buried feelings wrapped around the unfinished business of the past. The vulnerabilities of our child come rushing to the surface. Therefore, healing that wounded child within is vital. Not only in re-framing false belief systems and healing past trauma, but in tapping into their innocence and joy.

The Child Within Us

A child is born
A miracle in its creation
Such simple dignity
In oneness with the world
With a direct line to God

A tiny body in sweet perfection
Little hands, little feet
The delicate bit of skin around its ears
A celebration of life
Totally in tune with the universe

Its needs are so simple
Its desires so basic
In balance
Beginning life in purity
With the pure joy to succeed

Unafraid and authentic
This child finds the world
All around it an adventure
Talking to trees and teddy bears
Taking the time to listen
To hear and feel the stories they have to tell

Isn't it a shame
This innocence soon gone
And we grow up
All tangled in the shoulds and woulds
We lose the oneness and focus
We lose this pure fun of living

The pressures of our days
Scramble our hearts
We become out of balance
Out of oneness with the world
Too busy to take the time to play
Too busy to hold the truth

Wouldn't it be grand if
With the wisdom of our years
We could find again, that child
To find its clarity, its simplicity
This child has so much to tell us,
We are wise enough now to understand

SUGGESTED CHAPTER STUDY

- Think about your own past. What were some of the major events in your growing up that shaped who you are today? Both positively and negatively.

- Take the time to connect with your child within, whether it's comforting the scared and frightened child or enjoying their joy and energy. Not only a healing process for you, but it will bring a greater understanding and empathy in working with your clients and their wounded children.

CHAPTER TEN

STRUCTURE – THE GOALS AND INTENT

A good structure for any imagery must begin by exploring the goals and intentions of the therapist. Without a general understanding of what you want the imagery to accomplish and what a successful goal for finishing might be, there can be no structure.

The very first and possibly the most important goal of any imagery is to relax the client. For that, you must provide a safe environment. That means feeling safe with the therapist, often in a darkened room, in a comfortable chair. As we mentioned before, never do a first imagery without establishing a relationship of warmth and acceptance, non-judgment and openness. Show the client your sincere interest in them as a person, your belief in the power of imagery as a healing process, an assurance that there is nothing to fear and there is no wrong way to do an imagery. They won't be judged, and you might add the request that they in turn not judge their own performance. Whatever happens is ok.

As a therapist, your belief in the process of imagery can be vital in establishing not only a good rapport with the client, but also, provide the client with optimism that this process will work. Since the placebo is about 60% to 70% effective, share with the client some of the research proving that heart rate goes down, pulse and blood pressure lowers, the immune system, as well as the metabolism, are stimulated, and so on. Perhaps share some anecdotal stories about imagery. With your excitement, you can lay the groundwork for the client's belief that it will work, and together you can create miracles. The effectiveness of an imagery experience would obviously decrease if the therapist started out with, "I don't know if this will work, but let's give it a try."

Once the imagery begins, we go back to relaxation as the first goal. As you discovered in the chapter on the induction, quiet music and the soft, reassuring voice of the therapist prepares the way. Your relaxation in the induction begins to entrain the client to your quiet energy and brings them to the Alpha state; where it all begins. Remember, if all that happens in the entire imagery is 15-20 minutes of relaxation, you've done a good job for the client. That's a lot. We recommend that you choose to just introduce a pleasant, relaxing experience for the first time without any deep probing.

The next step is one of gathering information. Whether you're dealing with a symptom, a person, symbol or situation, ask a lot of questions. Encourage the client to share in great detail what they are experiencing, what they see, feel and even smell. This is just information without judgment, for the purpose of clarity and understanding, nothing to do with right or wrong, good or bad. Say, for example, a client wants to work on a conflict with his son. In an imagery, being able to talk to the son and even 'become' the son brings new insight. Understanding what happened and why from the perception of each person involved, allows for less defensiveness and more options for change, resolution or reconciliation. Also, defusing a negative situation by gathering information without the usual blame or attack, brings clarity, such as, "Now I understand why I did that."

Therefore, the objectives of this process should always be:

- Solution
- Resolution
- Or, at least peace of mind

There are always three different ways of coming to an answer that will be positive for the client, no matter what happens. Remember each of us is only 50% of any conflict and we have little power over what the other person does.

Solution is just what it sounds like. In a marriage problem, they solve the issue or issues and save the marriage. That can often come from new information and correction of false belief systems. However it happens, the issue has been solved. Resolution is basically working out a compromise that is satisfactory for both parties. Negotiation until they can agree to disagree, or are both happy enough with what they decided upon to continue the relationship or modify it. Peace of mind. There are some core issues – belief systems and personal integrity – that cannot be compromised.

Also, one person may become stubbornly stuck in a power struggle and has to win, or both people just can't or won't change. You can't change your basic personality for another person; become more outgoing if you are shy or less hyper if you are a control freak. If your attempts for modifying self are not enough, at some point, the relationship must end.

Remember the imagery of the father who molested his daughter, apologized profusely and asked for forgiveness, but told her not to contact him because he hadn't and couldn't change? Peace of mind comes from simply accepting the reality of what is; allowing the consequences to happen, divorce ending any relationship, whatever, and not holding a grudge or blaming the other person. As long as you hold on to your anger and bitterness for not getting what you wanted, you remain a victim and give power over your feelings to the other person.

A solution, a resolution or at least a peace of mind or acceptance; these are the goals of any imagery and any relationship, for that matter. Always honor the symptom or symbol; whether it's a pain, a sub-personality, or a cancerous tumor, even one that comes in a hostile manner as an enemy saying, "Thank you for coming, we have much to learn from you, there is nothing to fear from us. We come in peace." Note the use of 'we' referring to you as the therapist and the client. This tends to disarm a defensive symbol that comes expecting to be blamed or attacked. They'll generally be more willing to listen once they feel you came to listen to them.

STRUCTURE FOR ANY IMAGERY – SEE A SYMBOL

As an example, a client is experiencing an emotional pain. It could be from a divorce, a lost job, any disappointment. In beginning the imagery, after the induction, a starting point could be to find the place where they are holding this pain in their body.

After that place is found, the therapist could ask:
What does it feel like?
What does it look like?
Let it take any kind of form.

The client may respond with the following:
It's in my stomach.
It feels heavy and solid, a burden.
It looks like a large rock, black and ugly.

Note the probing questions asked by the therapist to keep the experience going, the invitation to become the symbol, with an opportunity to heal. The following is the dialogue that could unfold:

What is your overall impression of this rock?
It's immoveable and angry.

What do you like best and least?
Best, there is a strange feeling of protection. Least, it hurts.

Can you become the rock?
Yes

What are you feeling as the rock?
I feel angry and powerful, in control.

Look back at yourself, the person, what do you feel about this person?
Weak and inadequate, afraid of confrontation.

What is the most important thing you want this person to know about you?
I'm angry that this person chooses to be a victim all the time.

What do you want from this person you're not getting?
To speak up and defend himself.

What's your purpose in the stomach?
He fears speaking up so I immobilize him in the stomach.

Would you be willing to work with him on this?
Maybe. I'll try

Become yourself again. How do you feel about what you just learned?
Surprised, but hopeful.

Would you like to show your appreciation to the rock?
Yes.

In your imagination, put your hands around the rock in your stomach and just hold it.
It feels heavy and cold, difficult to hold.

Send it love, from your heart, through your hands. Just send it love and watch and see what happens.
It's getting warmer and smaller, less heavy.

Now, imagine that I'm handing you a spray bottle of a magic or healing solution. This solution is made up of all the chemicals from your own body that knows exactly what you and the rock need for healing. Tell this to the rock as you spray it lovingly and generously. Watch and see what happens.
It's very small now and very light. The color has turned to blue. It feels good to hold.

Would you like to remove this rock from your stomach?
Yes.

Good. I'm not sure if you are ready to totally get rid of the rock now, but tell the rock that you've been working hard, and both you and the rock need a rest. Tell the rock you are going to place it on a shelf to your right, just for a time, so you both can feel what it's like to not be at odds with each other.
Ok, I've placed the rock on the shelf. We're both ok with this.

How does your stomach feel without the rock there?
Feels great!

What does the stomach look like now?
A little beat up and torn.

Spray it with the magic solution.
It looks all healed and pink.

Now, you have options. You can return the rock to your stomach if that feels necessary or you can come and visit the rock and work out a better method of dealing with stressful situations. It's up to you.

This is one example of the structure when used with a symbol in the body. We've tried to lay it out with sample dialogue so you can get a more complete picture of what often happens between therapist and client. Remember, removing something from the body is not rejecting it. Note when it was sent love and sprayed with the magic solution, the rock improved and changed. It was trying to protect the client in its own way. Visiting the rock can bring information and advice about how to handle fear, rather than just holding it like a rock in the belly.

What happens if the rock doesn't change with the love and the magic solution? Most of the time there is anywhere from small, tentative change to instant positive response. Once in a while, the rock or whatever the symbol, will change to something entirely different, such as a baby or a lovely flower and the client might choose to keep the new symbol in his body in this new and healed state. If there is no change that doesn't mean you or the client have failed. That's just new information. Talk to the rock to find out why it has chosen not to respond to this love and gift of healing. There could be many reasons, perhaps a lack of trust of the client's sincerity in wanting to change.

Many people are just not ready to let go of symptoms or illnesses because of the benefits they bring. Cancer, for instance, can bring a host of loving people to care for the person, perhaps for the first time in years. If healed, would these people and their love just suddenly disappear? Most of this is unconscious. People have been known to say, "I'm dying for someone to love me," and not hear the obvious, but hidden message. Many clients over the years were reluctant to have a total recovery from an accident for fear of losing their disability payments, saying, "What if the pain comes back in six months or I can't find a job?"

We had a client years ago who was suffering with pancreatic cancer. In one of our first imageries together, he saw the cancer as a dog, a very friendly, lovable creature, playing in a beautiful meadow. At the end of the experience, we asked him if he would like to let the dog go free or take it back into his body, where it came from. Symbolically, it would indeed be more healing to release the dog, however, remember, no opinion of right or wrong. So, in asking this question, make sure you make the suggestion with no judgment. The dog jumped back into his stomach.

In subsequent imageries, this dog continually returned, but eventually my client was able to leave the dog in the meadow, with the promise to return. Obviously, there was a lot more information to gather. Imagery after imagery, this dog became an expected character in all his experiences. Then, in one imagery, we were dealing with some memories from his past, and we both were very aware that the dog never appeared. In the dialogue after the imagery, we knew the significance, and we both wept.

Any information gathered in an imagery experience that brings clarity to the client about the hidden or buried reasons for an illness or behavior is not to be judged as good or bad, just good information that can help provide options for change or new reasons for not wishing to change. One man in an imagery session saw a huge wall blocking his path to success. In a post imagery talk with the therapist, he accidentally said 'wife' instead of 'wall'. His unconscious revealed the real issue. He didn't choose to get a divorce because of many reasons personal to him, but by knowing the truth of what was blocking him, the symptoms he was suffering reduced greatly.

Let's do a little different version now, outside the body. We'll give you more of a skeleton outline and you fill in your own dialogue. As you read this, we would suggest you write down what you see as you follow the structure. Take your time to stop after each suggestion and experience what you see, feel and sense.

QUICK IMAGERY
THE PAINTING

See a painting. Describe the painting in some detail, size, shape, subject matter, colors, frame.

Where it is hanging?

Overall impression. What feelings and impressions come up?

What do you like best and least? There is always a best and least, that's different from good and bad.

Become the painting.

How do you feel as the painting?

Look back at yourself, the person, what are your feelings about the person?

Make a statement to the person.

Become yourself again.

How do you feel about your experience as the painting?

What did it say to you?

You can change the painting in any way that you want or leave it the way it is.

You can put the painting anywhere you want or leave it where you found it.

Now, slowly come back.

Did you experience the painting? What was the general theme of the picture you saw? What meaning does this have for what's going on in your life right now? Did you like the painting or not? If you did like it, what feelings came from the painting? Did you like it because it was, perhaps, a meadow that brought you a great sense of peace and relaxation, which you could use right now, or because it was vibrant and colorful and energized you?

If you had negative feelings about the subject matter or the colors, how does that fit in with your life in the moment? The symbols all have meaning. Our job as client or therapist is to search for these hidden messages. Can you see how this very simple skeletal outline can be used in any situation with any client, regardless of the subject matter? Your questions can vary and the subjects will be different, but the direction can follow the same purpose. We almost always ask the client to become the symbol they are looking at and to feel what the symbol is feeling. The purpose of this is empathy, walking in someone else's shoes, experiencing the other person's point of view, even if it is different from your own, especially if it's different.

Often we have had clients in an imagery see, for example, a furious lion that represents their angry and abusive father. We ask them to become the lion and the answer is, "No, I don't want to be like him or feel his evil passions. Why would I subject myself to that?" Because it could help understand father's anger, the source of this anger and therefore better understand the pain and frustration that causes him to react in this manner. It might even create feelings of sorrow for his pain, rather than fear or hatred for the man.

You shall know the truth and the truth shall set you free. Even uncomfortable truth sets us free. Just knowing that's the way it is, we have to learn to live with that information and stop trying to change it or deny it. This can bring a sense of closure and acceptance. This is not acceptance of a father's terrible behavior, but acceptance that we can't change someone else, so stop trying to do so and focus on what's best for us in this or any situation.

The surprising thing is that at least half the time, the client becomes the father or lion and feels fear, not anger. What a revelation when they say, "It never occurred to me that dad was afraid of anything and especially not me. As the lion, I felt threatened and terrified; afraid this person would reject me, hurt me or even kill me." Knowing that father was angry at the world and felt terrified and inadequate had nothing to do with the client. This helped to not take it so personally, rather than feeling at fault. Father acted the way he did because of his feelings about himself, not his child. One new perception of this kind can change a life forever.

In any imagery, gathering information is the objective. Keep asking questions. Invite the client to become the symbol, which provides empathy and perhaps a new perspective, and affords the opportunity for growth and change. Honor all symbols with no judgment. They come with valuable information and wisdom, even the scary ones. You'll be amazed how the statement such as, "We come in peace," can calm the most threatening monster.

In the first imagery we provide in our book, *Inner Peace—Outward Power, Guided Imagery to Use with the 12 Steps to Recovery,* we invite the listener to meet the pure addictive part of them. See that person. We continue the imagery with, "We honor you, we thank you, and in some way you have indeed saved this person's life. We want to listen to you." In doing this imagery with many clients in recovery, this was a revelation for them. The thought of honoring that part of them that had created such chaos and pain, was powerful. To listen to the needs of this addict and understand the motives can bring about change. Through imagery, provide the addict with new and different ways of behaving and coping.

In the Zen philosophy, there is a saying, *A million miles between the head and the heart*. The head gets it for the need to change or quit drinking or whatever, but until it reaches the heart, change is almost impossible. And imagery is that dialogue between the head and the heart; the magical road between two worlds. Remember, the addict part, the angry part, the fearful part, are all parts of us and we can never destroy a part of us. Our intent through the imagery process is to afford the opportunity to listen to the feelings and needs of each of these parts and hopefully bring them closer to center on that continuum of balance.

THE WISDOM OF CARL JUNG

Recapping a bit, we've given you a number of imagery samples, including our structure and starting points. We think you can see a pattern immerging in creating the best imagery journey possible for the client. Again, we reiterate, according to Carl Jung, a visualization or imagery should include three parts:

- A sacred peaceful place
- A magical energy
- Transformational ritual

Jung's first criteria of creating a peaceful place is what we call the induction. Creating that first five minutes of initial relaxation is critical in beginning any imagery process; to provide the client with a feeling of peace and safety. The magical energy could be considered the invitation for the client to see a symbol, talk to the symbol, or become the symbol. Also, introducing a person to come into the imagery, a helper of sorts, such as a healer or wise person, can be powerful. More on that later.

And lastly, in every imagery experience, Jung suggests a transformational ritual. We expand on this to say, provide the client with the opportunity to heal, whether it's a ceremony, ritual or just using the magic solution. Provide the options to change or heal any symbol. Send it love and see what happens. Spray it with a magic solution and see what happens.

In imageries designed for physical healing, we sometimes invite clients to literally submerge their whole bodies in the magic solution to flush away poisons, toxins, or any pain. In imageries to heal or re-parent the wounded child within, we often conclude the experience with the suggestion to have a sacred ceremony of adopting this child.

SUGGESTED CHAPTER STUDY

- Using the template of the imagery outline, 'See a Symbol', creates a starting point and subsequent suggested questions for a client who is suffering with bouts of depression.

- In an imagery experience, a client sees his anger as a furious fire-breathing monster. After a number of probative questions to the monster, the client is asked to 'become' this monster. He refuses. As the therapist, what would you do?

CHAPTER ELEVEN

EXTRA TOOLS

We've given you a number of places to start an imagery. You can never go wrong with seeing an animal or symbol that represents the particular issue the client is working on, or asking, "Where in your body do they hold the pain or problem?" Below are additional ideas to help you set the stage and begin an experience. Remember, in a group imagery, you will be guiding the whole experience, using open ended statements and suggestions, allowing the listeners to create their own experiences. In a one-on-one, your main concern is only the starting point of where you begin. The client will unfold the adventure. Of course, in previous chapters we presented questions to ask to keep the imagery going, but basically, your job is just to follow the client.

REMEMBERED WELLNESS

The concept of 'remembered wellness' as discussed in Chapter One, can be a marvelous starting point for a client dealing with any physical disease or imbalance. After the induction, invite the client to:

See someone coming towards them.
As they come closer, you realize this is the healthy, strong you.
What do you look like?
How old are you?
How do you feel about this you?
How is this you responding to you?

You're now off and running to interact with this person, dialoguing and gathering information. The following questions could bring some interesting responses:

- What is the most important information you wish this person to know about you?
- What are the blocks that keep this person from achieving their goals?
- If you could change this person in any way you wanted, what would you do?

On a subconscious level, we all know what we need to do to stay healthy, so through imagery, we are beautifully reminded. At the end of this imagery, we often close the experience by asking the client to say good-bye to their remembered, healthy self, saying, "Look around. You realize they are gone. And then, from somewhere deep within, you hear a voice, your voice, saying I'm within you now."

This reinforces the theory of Dr. Benson that as we start thinking about a time when we were healthy, the body will start replicating all the same hormones, chemicals and increasing the immune system. Knowing this healthy person is within can bring a marvelous mind-body connection of renewed health and well being.

We're often asked what if the client has a chronic condition and has never experienced good health. You could ask the client to imagine what it would feel like if they were in perfect physical health:

Describe the person in great detail.
What is the expression on the face of this you?

What do you see in the eyes?

Become the person.

What are you feeling as this person right now?

You have given the client the opportunity to experience that within all of us is perfect health:

This healthy you can relieve your symptoms.

This healthy you can alleviate your pain and discomfort.

This healthy you can hold you in times of stress.

If all the client receives is a new way of relaxing and being less stressed, symptoms and pain can be relieved, and indeed, imagery has done a good job. In explaining this concept of 'remembered wellness', many of our students have challenged us, saying, "What happens if I remember a time when I felt healthy, but perhaps, something was going on negatively in my body that I didn't know about. Would that remembered image put me back in that place?" Our answer to that question is always the same. Trust the body. The body knows exactly what it needs to be healthy. We certainly don't consciously think about the enzymes needed to digest our food; the body does that all by itself. So, trust the body to know and recognize balance and health. Allow your subconscious and that connection to the body to direct you to that perfect state of health and well being.

A SACRED TEMPLE, CHAPEL OR ROOM

Begin an imagery by taking the client to a sacred place. Depending on the issue, inviting them to a healing temple and meeting a doctor, or perhaps a special room of knowledge and greeting a wise person, can create an environment as a springboard to enhance the experience.

We worked with a client who wanted to get pregnant. She and her husband had been trying with no success for almost eleven years. Her gynecologist found no evidence that either of them had any problem conceiving. In an imagery, we took her to a sacred temple of initiation; an initiation of motherhood. We asked her to see a feminine figure who welcomed her into a temple. Hanging on the wall of the temple were plaques reflecting the names of all the women who were ready to receive and invite a baby into their life. Was she ready to place her name on the wall? The stage was set and we just followed the client.

Through the experience, the client encountered a very frightened image of herself. We dialogued with this woman who said, "I'm afraid I won't be a good mother." We discovered another woman who said, "My sister and aunt have the same problem of not getting pregnant, I guess it's just an inherited thing and it won't happen for me either." Both these sub-personalities of her were indeed alive and well, with strong belief systems. We were able to talk with them, send them love and gradually change their perspectives. What would be some of the statements you would make, or questions you would ask these sub-personalities?

Another client was suffering from test anxiety. She had failed two previous attempts at taking her attorney bar exam, and with this final test, the pressure for her was excruciating. We invited her to go to a very sacred library, filled with all the knowledge, all the information she needed. She saw it immediately and was overwhelmed by all the books lining the walls. The dialogue went something like this:

How do you feel being in this library?
I feel so overwhelmed. There are so many books. It's overwhelming, so much to know!

You see someone coming to join you, the keeper of this library. Do you see this person?
Yes, a very old man is approaching.

How do you feel about him?
I like him. He seems so wise.

How is he responding to you?
He is greeting me warmly and invites me to sit down and join him.

How does that feel?
I feel very comfortable and not so overwhelmed.

The conversation between them continued in gentleness and camaraderie. He told her that all the information she needed for her exam was right here in this room, and it was available to her whenever she needed it. There was no need to feel overwhelmed. The wise one spontaneously gave her a gift to remember the experience. Here's the beauty of imagery and the power of our imaginations. If we had been directing the imagery, we would never have thought of this on our own, but the wise one gave her a gift, a pen; a magic pen that had all the answers. How perfect was that? We found out later, after our session, she bought a beautiful pen that she used for her test. And, yes, she passed with flying colors.

THE ALPHA TRIGGER

As introduced by Jose Silva in the 1970's, bringing together the tips of the thumb and first two fingers of either hand causes the mind to adjust to a deeper level of greater awareness. While in the Alpha brain-wave level of imagery, suggesting that you put your fingers together, or for that matter, any other physical gesture will be a physical cue for the brain to replicate that same feeling in an awake state that was experience when initiated in the imagery. This is basically the 'classic conditioned response' as researched by Dr. Ivan Pavlov in 1892 with his dogs and the ringing of a bell.

For example, during an imagery of balancing and relaxing the body, tell the client to put their fingers together. This will lock in that wonderful feeling that can be called upon at a later time. This is particularly useful in calming people before an important sales meeting, stress of heavy traffic or anxiety about an exam. Of course, the client can't go into an imagery state right before a test or while driving, however, by merely putting the fingers together, the body will recall and be calm just as it experienced in the imagery. The more this technique is done, the more powerful it becomes.

Pressing the thumb and two fingers together is just one alpha trigger. Any gesture that is suggested during an imagery experience works with the same effect. Discuss this concept with your client to see if there is another trigger they might be more comfortable with. We had a client who was dealing with the symptoms of Parkinson's disease. It was very painful and difficult for her to put her fingers together, so for her the gesture we created was crossing her arms on her chest. It works the same way.

We did a series of imageries for the varsity basketball team at a local university. The imagery was specifically designed to help the players focus and follow through with their free throws. At the end of the imagery we wanted to include an alpha trigger. Playing basketball is hardly a time to press your thumb and two fingers together! So, for them, the trigger was pressing the tongue on the roof of the mouth. After using the imagery during the season, their free throw stats increased by over 40% and a fringe benefit was that their overall game performance increased in other areas, as well.

Another imagery was requested to help the team prepare for the championship games and not clutch. We wanted to create a new trigger, so after many suggestions from the team and the coaches, we came up with a smile. Not only did the new alpha trigger work, but with all five guys smiling, it indeed intimidated the other team.

Many people ask, "If you use different triggers, will it confuse the subconscious?" Absolutely not. The trigger is merely a way to remind the body of the peace, relaxation and focus achieved during an imagery experience. The body will go back to that same place, no matter if the reminder is a smile or pressing the fingers together, or whatever. It really doesn't matter.

Make sure your client is in a good place when you suggest doing an alpha trigger. In facilitating a group imagery, your intent for the experience may be to create something peaceful and relaxing, but sometimes clients do go off on their own journey and perhaps, they find themselves in a tentative situation. For these clients, an alpha trigger at this point would not be advised. So, always caveat the suggestions of an alpha trigger with, "If you are in a good place, if you feel peaceful and calm," before you continue.

THE HEALING OR MAGIC SOLUTION

Much as been said about the use of the magic solution, here is a tool you can use in a myriad of ways:

- Spray or apply to any part of the body experiencing pain or discomfort.
- Spray or apply to any part of the body where a symbol has been removed.
- Spray or apply to any symbol, sending it love and healing.
- Can come in a variety of forms: a spray, a salve, a liquid to drink, or even a large pool to submerge the whole body.

The body can produce all the chemicals and hormones necessary to gain and maintain good health, both physically and emotionally. So, use the healing solution often and liberally.

THE OLD COAT

If your client wishes to release weight, or release anything for that matter, a place to start an imagery could be to suggest they are wearing a heavy, old coat:

See yourself wearing a heavy old coat.
Feel it, smell it, experience it.
Look in the pockets.
Dialogue with the coat.
Become the coat.
As the coat, look back at the person and make a statement to the person.
Is there anything you would like to change about the coat?

You can get some good information about the emotions wrapped around the issue. Invite the client to take the coat off and ask what they would like to do with it. What happens if the client doesn't want to take it off? Is that ok? Of course. Whatever happens is ok, but perhaps you could suggest spraying the coat with the magic solution to make it lighter, or even send it love. Be creative.

Another spin on the coat concept is the bag lady. Invite the client to see themselves carrying and burdened with all sorts of bags, parcels, suitcases, etc:

Slowly put all the parcels down.
How does that feel to lighten the load?
For just today, for just right now, there is one parcel that is calling your attention.
Open it.
Once the parcel is open, have a dialogue with whatever is inside, whether it's a person, a symbol or perhaps even a memory from the past.
Get as much information as possible.
Make peace with it.

SOUL RETRIEVAL

Through our lives, we have all lost parts of ourselves to trauma, to grief over the loss of a loved one, possibly to guilt and shame. Often, we feel empty, as if some of our parts have been stolen. We may feel hopeless, helpless, with no direction or goals. The body is often vulnerable to depression and open to physical imbalance. Many of your clients may come with similar symptoms. Not unlike some Native American cultures where the shaman will literally travel within someone's energy to reclaim these pieces, use imagery to find these lost parts.

One of the most powerful workshops we have ever facilitated was on this subject of 'Soul Retrieval'. In one of the imageries, we invited each participant to see three people from their past who had hurt or injured them in some way. One by one, we directed them to have a dialogue with each of these people, telling them how their actions had affected them and providing an opportunity for each person to respond, further suggesting that each of these people had taken or stolen a piece from them and it was time to return it.

It was a group imagery so we had no idea what the experiences were until the discussion that followed. It was amazing that most of the participants told us that the people they saw gladly returned the piece, or symbol, and in most cases were not even aware of taking it in the first place, and they sincerely apologized. Since all information processed through the brain is accepted, whether conscious or subconscious, as real, perhaps there was a healing; a forgiveness, a true soul retrieval.

Another variation on this same theme would be to have the client see someone approaching who needs to make an apology. Often, the person that appears comes as a surprise to the client, not realizing how much the experience had impacted their subconscious. Allow sufficient time for the client to explain their feelings, and also for the person to share. If the person asks for forgiveness, that's great; a solution or a resolution. If they are not remorseful, at least it's peace of mind that the client was able to share their feelings.

CIRCLE

Either at the beginning of an imagery to bring balance and a sense of grounding, or at the end of the imagery to create a ritual, have the client imagine a large circle drawn in the earth. Invite them to step into the circle and find the center. Since the circle is a powerful symbol of wholeness, self-love, confidence and self-esteem, plugging into that center can bring a real sense of personal empowerment. Often, we will invite other people to join the circle, standing on the circumference, offering love and support.

GIFTS

Another tool we often use is the exchange of gifts. At the appropriate time in an experience, invite the client to give the symbol, the person, the animal a gift, a token of their appreciation for the information they just received. Similar to sending it love, or spraying it with a magic solution, a gift can be a powerful gesture of healing. Likewise, have the symbol, the person, or the animal give a gift to the client. How powerful the gift of that magic pen was for our client, the attorney.

Also, after the imagery, in the discussion about the experience, it can be insightful to look at the symbolism of the gift; what is the universal meaning. Years ago, we had a client who was working on her issues of abandonment. In imagery, she received a gift from her spirit guide. It was a beautiful necklace that the guide, almost in ceremony, fastened around her neck. It was extremely touching and emotional for her. After the experience, we discussed the imagery and she asked, "What does necklace mean?" We didn't know at the time, but after some research, we found the answer.

In aboriginal culture, the ancient tradition was for each tribe to adorn themselves with a necklace that would symbolize and identify their particular group; the tiger tooth people, the huckleberry people. It was a powerful statement of belonging to a tribe. With this new insight, it brought even more meaning for our client.

THE NINE STEMS

Dr. Joseph E. Shorr, a clinical psychologist in Los Angeles, calls his approach *Psychoimagination* and is one of the most innovative imagery therapists in the world. We've had the privilege of knowing Joe for over twenty years and sitting in on many of his seminars. His book, *Go See the Movie in Your Head* is a fascinating read and has been a great resource for us. Shorr does imagery in a completely unique way. For example, we have used one of his imageries in our training, called 'The Painting'. He never used an induction or music.

He would simply say something like this:

Take a moment to center yourself.
Relax and close your eyes.
Find yourself in the lobby of a tall building.
You go down an elevator to the basement.
There you will see a covered painting on a wall.
Remove the cover and be aware of what you see, feel, think and do.
When you are done, open your eyes.

And people had great imageries! When we do this imagery, however, we use our own method of an induction to relax the group and then turn his instructions into a story line of about ten or fifteen minutes.

Shorr felt the universal meaning of the painting had to do with one's sexuality. Going down an elevator is going down inside self to one's animal or basic nature. We usually cover up our genitals or private parts and only reveal them to special relationships, so seeing a covered painting, according to Shorr, represents our sexuality. We have used this imagery with literally thousand of college students and clients over the years. College students tend to be more open about their sexuality. But, to be totally truthful, only about 10% saw something that they felt was sexual. Most of the people saw the painting in the same way that Leuner used the meadow; a view of what was going on in their lives at that moment. We always follow the client and their insight into meaning.

Shorr feels that the experience and subsequent questions that arise from the imagery should reveal five things:

- How you define yourself in relationships with others.
- How you feel others define you.
- The kinds of conflicts within you.
- If you are ready to face conflict.
- Shows how to resolve conflicts through the use of imagery.

To accomplish this, he created what he called 'The Nine Stems'. We introduce this now as a wonderful tool for exploring the five goals above. Joe would suggest that you 'become' the painting, or any symbol, and finish the stems as the symbol, spontaneously, with no time for thought:

- I feel
- The adjective that best describes me
- I wish
- I must
- I secretly
- I need
- I will
- I fear
- Never refer to me as

Can you see how these stems can reveal answers to the five goals he stated? 'I feel' and 'the adjective that best describes me' can certainly define self. The remaining stems tend to define how you feel about others and yourself, with each stem a slightly different approach. One of our clients went through the first five blissfully showing a strong love for people and a need to do for others, but 'I secretly', she blurted out, "I hate people!"

'Never refer to me as' is generally what we secretly fear we really are. For instance, 'never refer to me as a coward' might reveal a strong inward fear of being a coward, and we try hard to never show that side to others. Whatever negative trait we see in other people or have a strong aversion to, could reveal a part of us that has been totally repressed or denied, buried deep in the subconscious. Many will have no answer for 'I secretly'.

These stems can be used within an actual imagery experience, talking to a symbol or animal, or, as we have found with our own work with clients and students, asking these questions after the imagery is complete can also be profound. Invite your client to become the symbol again and ask away. It's amazing how insightful their responses can be. The answers create a wonderful backdrop for understanding the imagery and the symbol.

SUGGESTED CHAPTER STUDY

- Using Joe Shorr's 'The Nine Stems', go back to any of the quick imageries we have presented in the book and 'become' the symbol again. Whether it's becoming the animal that represents your spouse or partner, or perhaps the symbol that represents your anger, become that symbol right now and write down your answers. The faster you respond, the more the answers will come from your subconscious:

    - I feel
    - The adjective that best describes me
    - I wish
    - I must
    - I secretly
    - I need

- I will
- I fear
- Never refer to me as

- Using the concept of 'Soul Retrieval', create a basic starting point for a client who is working on issues of grieving the loss of their spouse. Write some subsequent suggestions and questions you would ask to keep the experience going. What would be the goal and intent for this experience?

CHAPTER TWELVE

HOW TO END THE IMAGERY

In writing and facilitating a group imagery, review your objectives of what you want to accomplish. Whether it's just a peaceful journey to meet a wise person or a more tentative adventure of meeting, for example, the angry part or the fearful part of self, make sure you have provided a full and rich experience. Always provide an opportunity for healing or change, and end on an optimistic note.

The full experience should be no more than 20 to 25 minutes in length. Since the brain cannot sustain this Alpha state of relaxation for more than 20 minutes, if you go much longer, the group will either fall asleep or wake up. With the one-on-one experience, there's no script beyond the induction. End when the imagery feels complete on some level, with a natural conclusion and a specific goal reached. Even though you are following the client, there should be a plan as to where you wish to conclude the experience.

During our seminars, we always demonstrate a one-on-one experience with a volunteer. Often the imagery will go 40 to 50 minutes. Since the client is dialoguing, there is no chance they will fall asleep, but it's amazing that you can almost set your watch at 20-minute intervals of when the client will start to come out of the Alpha state. If this happens, you'll know it. The client will start to talk a little faster and perhaps even louder. Merely instruct them to relax, take a deep breath and continue on. It's that easy. The dance between the Beta and Alpha brain-waves is effortless.

In previous chapters we have provided tools to facilitate your use of time and come to a logical and positive conclusion. Always try to end with an encouraging remark that something important happened that was an improvement in the client's life. Even if you felt you didn't accomplish what you had intended, you might say, "We have learned a lot of new information to think about today and perhaps this would be a good place to stop for now and we can pick it up next week."

In bringing a one-on-one imagery to a close, always summarize what the client experienced and the information gained. An example could go something like this:

Slowly, start your journey back to this room.
Remembering your place of peace.
Remembering the wise person you met.
The animal that represented your father.
The dialogue you had with him.
The information you learned.
Remembering the gifts you exchanged.
Remembering it all, start to come back to this room.

It's important that you review the experience. This is helpful for the client to remember the events, but also for you, as the therapist. It's also a powerful statement to the client that you were listening, involved and participating. Similarly, in bringing a group imagery to a close, recap the whole experience you provided for the listeners.

In the script for 'The House' imagery, which is located in the Appendix, the bring-back outlines the whole adventure:

And, now, slowly you walk away from the house.
Remembering everything.
Remember the person that greeted you.

The living room, the dining room, the kitchen.
Your impressions of the bedroom and bathroom.
Remembering the image you saw in the mirror.
The attic and also what was the item you brought downstairs.
Where you placed it.
Remembering any changes you made to the house.

And, whether it's a one-on-one or a group imagery, close the experience with instructions to come back to this room:

- Slowly, start your journey back to this room.
- Wiggle your toes.
- Wiggle your fingers.
- Take a deep breath.
- Reinforce the alpha trigger, if it was used in the experience.
- Feeling alive, awake, renewed, refreshed.
- And when you're ready, you can open your eyes.
- Welcome back.

During this bring-back process above, make sure you raise your voice a bit, speaking a little bit louder. Giving permission to open their eyes is important as many people will not do so until you say it. We cannot stress enough the importance that, when the client does open their eyes, you are fully alert and focused on them. There is a sacred element of trust and comfort necessary for your client to allow you to facilitate the process of imagery with them. Being connected and alert in that moment makes a beautiful empathetic and sincere statement of, "I'm right here. I support you. I have journeyed with you."

Remember, we said that it takes the average brain about 5 minutes to reach the Alpha brain-wave place. Conversely, it takes about 15 minutes to completely return to the awake and aware state of Beta. After the imagery has concluded, provide some time to allow your client to come back fully. This is an excellent time to discuss the imagery and perhaps look at what some of the symbols could represent, which adds richer meaning to the whole experience.

In doing imagery, we can analyze the symbols and parts of the experience similar to interpreting a dream. In the Appendix, we have provided a directory of some of the more common symbols and their universal meanings. Universal symbols share the collective energy and consciousness of our world, and how certain images tend to represent and bring up certain feelings and meanings. However, particular symbols are those interpretations that are uniquely an individual's belief or history.

For instance, the smell of chicken soup for someone might bring up a host of scary and fearful memories of being in the hospital as a child and being served soup. However, the universal symbol for chicken soup is that of personal nourishment. When there is a contradiction between the universal symbol and the particular symbol, you must go with the particular symbol. An imagery is a client's personal journey into their subconscious and their beliefs, and therefore, their connection and meaning is the most important.

In discussing an imagery experience with your client, suggest what the universal meaning of a particular symbol in the experience tends to mean, and see if they resonate with the interpretation. More times than not, it fits and some great insight is uncovered. If they don't resonate with your analysis, you must go with the interpretation of the client. This is the client's journey, not yours.

Know your symbols. They can be a great place to begin an imagery. For example, perhaps your client comes to you wanting to work on exploring the masculine and feminine aspects within them. Knowing the symbolism of the sword and the vase, our masculine and feminine aspects, you may invite them to see a sword and experience it. Have them see a vase and experience it. And then, have the sword and the vase make statements to each other. Much information and insight can be gained. Another example may be that your client is working on issues of feeling alone and not supported in the world. We know that the necklace is a symbol of belonging; being a part of the tribe.

At some point in the imagery you may want to suggest the following:

You are given a necklace. Do you see it?
Yes, I see it right now.

In the imagery, never say, the necklace is a universal symbol of belonging and feeling protected. Instead, you may wish to ask the following questions:

What does this necklace look like?
Would you like to put it on?
How does it feel to wear it?

Be mindful not to tell the client the universal meaning of a symbol before they begin the imagery. This will definitely contaminate the experience. Allow the adventure to just unfold. There will be plenty of time after the experience to discuss the possible universal meanings.

Perhaps your client comes to you wanting to just experience the process of imagery and do some personal exploration. A house is a powerful symbol of self and having the client explore it can be very revealing. Don't say to the client, "Let's do an imagery and explore a house that represents self, with each room representing a different aspect within." Merely guide the client through the various rooms, asking what they see, what they feel, etc. Interpreting the meaning of each of the rooms should not be done until after the experience and after the client has shared their interpretations. Never interpret a symbol while a client is still in the experience.

What animal do you see?
I see a rabbit coming towards me.

Your remarks should not be that this rabbit represents creativity, fertility and new life. The rabbit will give you all the information you need. Allow the client to have the experience without the contamination of knowing its universal meaning. Suggest, but don't modify or define any symbol in a client's imagery.

You see before you a glass bottle filled with a magic solution for healing. What color is it?
Yes, I see it, and it's red.

Knowing the symbolism of colors, don't say, "Change that color to green." Even though green is a powerful color of healing, for the client the information that red will bring can be very meaningful and important. Since red is the color for passion and anger, perhaps the insight gained will be about an old anger that needs to be explored, resolved or healed. Or maybe, the imagery could be telling the client to have more passion about their healing. Never change a symbol or image for the sake of your own value of improvement.

See an animal that represents your mother.
I see a wild, vicious bear who wants to eat me.

Perhaps your first instinct would be to change that bear to a friendlier animal. But, there is much to be learned from the angry, hungry bear. Just listen. We've found that it's actually a lot more exciting to talk to the angry, belligerent creatures. They always have so much passion. You may want to ask some of the following questions:

How do you feel about the bear?
What do you like most about the bear?
What do you like least about the bear?
Become the bear.
How do you feel as the bear?
You may wish to have a conversation with the bear.
Suggest that the bear look back at the person, the client.
How do you feel about this person?
What do they want to tell this person?

Only after you have explored the bear, or whatever symbol, in its original form, can you even suggest that it change. After honoring and getting information from the animal, you could ask the following questions:

Is there anything you would like to change about this bear?
Send the bear love.
Watch what happens?

If the bear doesn't change, that's ok. What have you learned? If the bear does change, allow it to just happen.

In the post-talk after the imagery, don't start to analyze or interpret the imagery until the client has finished sharing their experience and what they feel it means. Only at this point can you start to suggest and interpret the possible meanings. If you start to interpret too soon, you may contaminate the client's interpretation and what they wish to share with you. If in this post-talk, the client is talking about the kitchen in 'The House' imagery, if they are told that it represents how they nurture themselves or were nurtured in childhood, the client's judgment may get in the way and they may neglect to tell you some of the negative details, for fear of being judged by you.

Try not to judge the symbols within an imagery. Remember, the information gained in the experience is just information. There is no right symbol or wrong symbol. It's just a symbol with rich information to share with us. Without judgment, our responses should always be, "That was interesting," rather than, "That was good or bad."

After an imagery, if your client becomes very emotional, passionate or feels incomplete about something they saw or experienced, you can always take them back into the imagery. Since it takes awhile for the client to return fully to the awake state, just a few suggestions from you can return them to the scene. This is a particularly useful tool when doing imagery with a group. During the discussion after the experience, if someone feels unsettled or unfinished on some level, take them back to finish the experience or get more information.

PATTI: Years ago I facilitated a quarterly Imagery group for women going through breast cancer at our local hospital. Each meeting, I did a different imagery for healing. One of the imageries I did was inviting everyone to see a healer and experience a marvelous pool filled with a magic solution, to flush away all the toxins and poisons in their bodies.

Everyone had a great experience except one woman, Sandi, who was obviously very emotional after the imagery. I asked her what she was feeling and she told the group that during the experience, she saw her mother standing next to the pool. She felt like there was something her mom wanted to say, but she suddenly disappeared. Sandi went on to say she had lost her mother just a few years earlier to breast cancer. I asked her permission to take her back into the scene, she agreed and I invited her to be back in the magic pool, enjoying herself. I then invited mom to come back.

Sandi, do you see your mother?
Yes, she's standing right where I saw her before.

How do you feel just seeing her now?
She looks so happy and beautiful.

What would you like to say to her?
I love you and I miss you. I'm so sorry you had to go through all that you did.

How is your mother responding to your words?
She's smiling and she's now in the pool with me.

How does that feel?
It's so wonderful to be with her again.

Is there something your mom would like to say to you?
She's saying that she is so sorry I have to go through this, but, she knows that I will be ok. She will always be there to protect me and I don't have to die.

Perhaps in that moment, a belief system was changed; changed from, "If I get cancer, I will die like my mother," to a new, empowering belief of, "I will survive. I will thrive." Remember the brain doesn't know the difference between what's real and what's imagined. And since the body is a faithful, obedient servant, we can change the messages we have programmed ourselves to believe.

To recap, the full imagery session should include:

- The Pre-Talk – Getting to know your client or group, establishing a rapport
- Induction – The Relaxation
- The Body – The Adventure
- The Bring-Back – Recapping the Experience
- The Post-Talk – Discussing the Experience

HOW MUCH TIME TO ALLOW FOR A FULL IMAGERY EXPERIENCE

It is imperative to allow at least 15 minutes for a pre-talk before the imagery starts, to discuss the issues before you dive in. If the client or group is not familiar with the concept of imagery, this is a good time to explain the process and perhaps show them how easy it is. At this point, you may, without even doing an induction, invite them to see a horse, describe the horse and how they relate to the animal. Simple and quick. There's no right way or wrong way to do it.

Then you need at least 15 minutes after the imagery to talk about what happened, summarize their experience and give time for the client to be fully back in an awake state. It has been researched that it only takes two or three minutes for the client to come to a place of opening their eyes, but it might take another 10 minutes more before they should leave your office and drive their car home. If you are working with 50-minute sessions, this would leave 20 minutes for the actual imagery. This is usually sufficient time for an imagery, but it can run a few minutes more or less. You do the math and decide how long your sessions should be.

If you are constrained by the clock and you're in an imagery and running out of time, with only 15-20 minutes before you have to close, you might say to the client:

We are short on time.
We have to wrap this up soon.
How would you like to bring this to a conclusion?
What would you like to do to complete this experience?

When we do imagery with clients, we like to work in two-hour sessions. This affords plenty of time to accomplish our goals. Often, we prefer to go over the imagery in detail in a following session, and just do a short overview at the end of the imagery. We invite the client to go home and write down their experience, knowing it will be discussed in great detail the next time we meet.

SUGGESTED CHAPTER STUDY

- Create, using your own words, a final bring back to end any imagery experience.

- For the therapist, taking notes during an imagery experience can be very helpful, especially in recapping the experience at the end of the imagery. However, make sure when you say, "You may open your eyes," your pen is down and you are open, receptive and connected with your client.

CHAPTER THIRTEEN

PSYCHOSYNTHESIS

CHUCK: Now that we have shared our structure, goals and intent for creating both group and one-on-one imageries, I would like to share the theoretical framework that supports and defines this approach. While I prefer to think of myself as more eclectic than locked into one simple theory in my 40 years of doing imagery, I have drawn from many people along the way. However, there is a basic theory that most closely stands for all I believe in and practice, both in my work and in the way that I choose to live my life.

Three books helped shape my career in psychology in the early stages. Interestingly enough, all were originally published the same year, 1955: *The Art of Loving*, by Eric Fromm, *Man's Search for Himself,* by Rollo May and *Toward a Psychology of Being,* by Abraham Maslow. All of them were transpersonal psychologists who, although influenced by Freud, were strong believers in the mind-body connection, even before that was a popular concept and the spiritual nature that was beyond the personal. Other heroes of mine have been covered in the book, but these men inspired me with their beliefs and I used these three books as texts when I first started teaching. And they are still classics today.

I come from a background of depth psychology, where the issue has always been to root out the source of the dysfunction and heal it, rather than the more modern approach of symptom removal as the solution, which can be accomplished more quickly, without going back to correct the past. The latter, the behavior modification approach, is very effective for children and teenagers and those who don't respond well to insight therapy. Understanding why we do what we do as a method of changing may be too painful or take too long. I agree with Leuner and DeSoille that, *Guided imagery is a superior short term therapy that closes the gap between symptom-centered procedures and the great psychoanalytical cure.*

In my own personal therapy, while in my Master's Degree program before becoming a therapist, I learned guided imagery from my own therapist, Paul Fairweather, PhD, who called it visualization. This had a profound impact on my personal growth. Later, I was privileged to meet and study with Robert Gerard, PhD, someone I came to admire greatly. Gerard was a Frenchman who was Paul's therapist and a friend of Robert DeSoille, and was one of a handful of people from Europe who brought guided imagery to the United States in the 1950's. It was Gerard who introduced me to the work of Roberto Assagioli, MD, an Italian psychiatrist. Through his books, *Psychosynthesis* and *Act of Will,* Assagioli's theory of Psychosynthesis has become the basis of our work ever since.

Assagioli developed the concept of Psychosynthesis to explore sub-personalities. Combining the dynamics of Psychosynthesis and guided imagery provide a powerful tool to affect an integrated and fully functioning human being in all of us. The more integrated and fully functioning a person is, the more apt they are to attract a similar whole, healthy person to share a relationship. This approach, because it is both holistic and spiritual, deals with the entire person and acknowledges the higher consciousness of innate spirituality within. Additionally, Psychosynthesis values rather than judges all parts of self, even those sub-personalities that most of us disown, hate or consider being negative or evil.

The two guided imagery therapists, Hanscarl Leuner and Robert DeSoille, were later additions to my learning and training in imagery. In all my experiences with hundreds of people who use imagery in their work, it has been very gratifying to discover that what we do and teach in IntraPersonal imagery is most commonly aligned with DeSoille and Leuner. Adding some contemporary heroes, and perhaps surprisingly, they come from the world of science rather than psychotherapy: Gregg Braden, *Spontaneous Healing of Belief* and *Fractal Time,* Bruce Lipton, *Spontaneous Evolution* and *The Biology of Belief* and Candace Pert, *Molecules of Emotion* and her audio presentation, *Your Body is Your Subconscious.*

PSYCHOSYNTHESIS

This theory most closely blends with our own spiritual, practical and balanced beliefs about functioning from the essence of the true self and being the person you were born to be. According to Assagioli:

- Values times of darkness as much as joy and enlightenment.
- Emphasizes the importance of using obstacles as steps to growth rather than promising their disappearance.
- Opts for doubting and risking rather than guaranteed safety and ecstasy.
- Prefers the creativity of confusion to the deceptive clarity of ready-made answers.
- Reminds us of effort, as well as effortlessness.
- Acknowledges the immense variability of human beings. There is no standard result.
- Praises the unexpected event that shatters in one moment our model of how it all should be.

Psychosynthesis values rather than judges events and issues of our lives. Whenever we refuse to judge things as black or white, right or wrong, moral or immoral, we have reached another dimension of thought. Judging keeps us in that turmoil of conflict between sides, rather than looking at every issue for its own truth and reason for existence. What can we learn from this? Roberto Assagioli's dis-identification and self-identification exercise may be his most significant contribution to understanding the concept of self and the meaning of Psychosynthesis.

IDENTIFICATION EXERCISE
ROBERTO ASSAGIOLI

I HAVE a body, but I am NOT my body. My body may find itself in different conditions of health or sickness, it may be rested or tired, but that has nothing to do with my self, my real 'I'. I value my body as my precious instrument of experience and of action in the outer world, but it is only an instrument. I treat it well, I seek to keep it in good health, but it is not my SELF. I HAVE a body, but I AM NOT my body.

I HAVE emotions, but I am NOT my emotions. My emotions are diversified, changing, sometimes contradictory. They may swing from love to hatred, from calm to anger, from joy to sorrow, and yet my essence – my true nature – does not change. 'I' remain. Though a wave of emotion may temporarily submerge me, I know that it will pass in time; therefore, I am not this emotion. Since I can observe and understand my emotions, and then gradually learn to direct, utilize, and integrate them harmoniously, it is clear that they are not my SELF. I HAVE emotions, but I AM NOT my emotions.

I HAVE a mind, but I am NOT my mind. My mind is a valuable tool of discovery and expression, but it is not the essence of my being. Its contents are constantly changing as it embraces new ideas, knowledge, and experience. Often it refuses to obey me! Therefore, it cannot be me, my SELF. It is an organ of knowledge of both the outer and the inner worlds, but it is not my SELF. I HAVE a mind, but I AM NOT my mind.

I HAVE desires, but I am NOT my desires. Aroused by drives – physical and emotional – and by outer influences, desires too are changeable and contradictory, with alternatives of attraction and repulsion. I HAVE desires, but they are not myself.

After dis-identifying myself from the contents of consciousness, such as sensations, emotions, thoughts, I RECOGNIZE AND AFFIRM THAT I AM A CENTER OF PURE SELF-CONSCIOUSNESS, A CENTER OF WILL. As such, I am capable of observing, directing, and using all my psychological processes and my physical body.

Who am I then? I am the permanent factor in the ever-varying flow of my personal life. I am that which has a sense of being, of permanence, of inner balance. I am a center of identity and pure self-consciousness. I AFFIRM MY IDENTITY AS THIS CENTER.

I recognize and affirm that as this center I have not only self-consciousness, but also creative, dynamic power, I recognize that as this center, I can learn to observe, direct, and harmonize all the psychological processes and the physical body. I will to achieve a constant awareness of this fact in the midst of my everyday life, and to use it to give increasing meaning and direction to my life.

I AM A CENTER OF IDENTITY, SELF-CONSCIOUSNESS AND WILL

Within us all is a 'true self', which Psychosynthesis refers to as the 'transpersonal self', which is a blend of individuality and universality. This deep integrity or God-like awareness in consciousness knows absolute truth. The 'transpersonal self' knows all the problems and can provide all the solutions for our well being. We do not have to be in touch with this 'true self' in order to function in the world. We can shower, dress, drive and perform most of our daily tasks without engaging the brain, let alone the 'true self' or 'transpersonal self'. What we do need, however, is our 'true self' on call and available as needed, with a minimum of distraction and distortion from our many defensive parts. Unfortunately, very few people have that easy access to the 'true self' when necessary or needed.

Therefore, most of us function from a place of identification with one of the various parts or sub-personalities within us, such as fear, anger, rebellion, conformity or judgment. These parts take over and temporarily run our lives. They are semi-autonomous and often contradictory, creating conflict within us. Much of the self-actualization of Psychosynthesis is concerned with finding, recognizing and harmonizing these sub-personalities into an integrated, loving, internal family unit.

To illustrate this actualization process further, one of our clients, Marge, came to therapy to work on two general issues. She wanted to lose twenty pounds and become more comfortable with her femininity. She felt that guided imagery could help. Marge had an attractive face and rather stocky body. She dressed in a conservative, businesslike style and was indeed a successful executive. In one of our first sessions she came in waving a dictionary, proclaiming why she didn't want to be more feminine. Webster's second definition under feminine was 'weak' and she had no desire to be weak or vulnerable. I pointed out that saying feminine is weak is like saying my watch is weak because it can't defend me in a fight. It was designed to tell time, not to fight, and if it functions well, it is, therefore, strongly doing its job. Feminine is soft, receptive, loving and caring. To do that well is not weak.

It was decided to work with imagery and her sub-personalities and this was done over a period of six months. In a relaxed state, an invitation was made for a sub-personality to take symbolic form and appear. She saw a solitary but beautiful, deep burgundy rose, tightly closed and perched on a single stalk in a field. One could assume that this was her femininity, but she called it her beauty. Her beauty was fully developed, but closed to protect it in this vulnerable open field. The obvious goal would be for her beauty to open up to be seen and related to. This task was not easy. From previous experience, Marge had developed intense fear of being hurt.

Marge could not open the rose in her vulnerability, her open field. A safe environment was needed, so it was suggested that she put a fence around the rose. Eventually the beautiful flower blossomed. People came and admired and took care of the rose. Nothing bad happened. If something negative had appeared, it would have been worked with to see what it symbolized in her life. She was asked to repeat this imagery daily, and in a short time Marge became more feminine, more open with people, letting her beauty shine.

In ensuing weeks, Marge's imagery discovered and uncovered many sub-personalities. She found a little girl that needed to be mothered, a wise old man who represented her masculine wisdom, giving her advice and direction, a prostitute who needed love to mend some of her sexual hang-ups, and a wall of fat that was her protection. Psychosynthesis states, *When we are no longer helplessly controlled by these sub-personalities, we can bring them under the conscious direction of the personal or 'true self'.* The way to break free of being helplessly controlled by these sub-personalities is to dis-identify from them. If we can detach or dis-identify from each individual sub-personality, such as anger or fear, we are then free to identify with the 'true self'. We will expand on this concept in the next chapter.

An interesting way of perceiving our various sub-personalities is to think of them as rejected and rebellious children. Psychotherapist Hal Stone, in his book, *Embracing Ourselves,* reminds us that there are primary selves that are not rejected and indeed run the show. This theory is less concerned with the parts that work well, but more involved with the disowned or rebellious ones. If it works, don't fix it. What happens to a rejected child who feels unloved? He turns on the one who rejects him. The two extremes are rebellion or withdrawal, either one of which can drive parents crazy.

What occurs when a part of us feels rejected or unloved? In exactly the same manner as the parent/child interaction, it can turn on us, creating behavior patterns of rebellion or withdrawal. Either one of these extremes creates issues for us, as well as a spouse or partner. As an example of a rebellious sub-personality, Jane had a dream she was a monk, a spiritual leader, being choked by a monster. She woke up very frightened and confused. In an imagery experience, we completed the dream. The monk asked the monster, "Who are you and why are you choking me?" The monster replied, "I am your anger. You reject me and don't see my value. I'm the one who protected you from your mother and a hostile world, and now you reject me, so I'm going to kill you!"

It is not difficult to conclude that Jane was a spiritual and religious person who saw all anger, her own as well as others, as evil and bad. As a result, she became nice, generous and passive. Of course, she was constantly taken advantage of and hurt. Her anger built up inside her and finally erupted. When it came out in explosions of viciousness and profanity, Jane was shocked and disgraced, proving her theory that anger was evil and bad.

Anger, however, is not moral or immoral, it's just anger. How you express it determines the moral value. Anger is also energy, power, and protection. If used constructively to care for one's self, it will not build to extreme explosions. The constructive use of anger entails keeping normal anger normal, assertively expressing one's feelings in an appropriate manner as they are being experienced, such as, "I am feeling very uncomfortable, angry, upset, confused, or defensive with what is happening now and I need to talk about it." Most of us feel we don't have the right to do that, or we might hurt someone's feelings, or start a fight. So we repress the anger. Eventually, the anger builds to the point where we don't care about possible consequences, and we now feel justified to overreact.

Psychosynthesis teaches five phases of harmonization for working with sub-personalities. These are tools that can help us identify and deal with all our various sub-personalities, creating honest and appropriate behavior, not only within ourselves, but with our partners and friends. Speaking our truth is the highest level of our personal empowerment. Finding out and honoring what our truth is, that's the hard part. The clues to our authenticity may be held or even possibly hidden by one or more of our sub-personalities. Honor and get to know them all. In their balance, they indeed hold our truth.

FIVE PHASES OF HARMONIZATION
RECOGNITION

The first step is to look for the sub-personalities. They are there. To recognize someone is more than saying, "I know who you are." The United States recognizes the government of Germany means that we acknowledge their right to exist and represent their people. A statement like, "The speaker recognizes the Senator from California," means the speaker gives the Senator the right to speak on the floor. We must give legitimacy to all our sub-personalities; their right to exist and express themselves openly in the total spectrum of self, and honor their appropriateness in our lives.

Sometimes sub-personalities will appear as monsters and give hostile or negative responses, such as, "I want total control, or I want to kill you." We often become defensive or scared. Imagine your seven year old brother saying he wants to kill you. Rather than accepting the challenge in defense, what if you replied, "How would your life be different if I were dead?" You acknowledged his right to be angry, asked how you are disrupting his life, and why he is angry with you. He might possibly reply with, "There would be more time, attention, and money for me. I could have your room." Now you know what the real issues are, and you are able to address his true needs for attention and love, rather than anger and defensiveness. You honored his right to be angry.

ACCEPTANCE

This comes gradually. There is a lack of trust on both sides. We have rejected the sub-personality because it is a part of us we don't like or are ashamed of. We fear that by accepting this part of us, we'll give it permission to be destructive, and that we are condoning negative behavior. We feel if it's ok to accept anger, we might kill. If it's ok to accept submissiveness, we won't be strong. However, the sub-personality is acting out in an exaggerated extreme because it feels rejected.

As mentioned in a previous chapter, every parent knows it's difficult to love the rebellious child. How can this be done? It's accomplished by separating the child from his behavior. The parent says, "I love you, but this behavior is not acceptable. I love you enough to do whatever it takes to keep you from destroying yourself and our family." Once the child feels loved and accepted, there is no further need to be rebellious or hurtful, and behavior becomes appropriate.

CO-ORDINATION

The next step is the development and improvement of the specific sub-personality. Psychosynthesis believes in an absolute truth or premise that is essential to this work and is somewhat unique to psychotherapy. Quoting Assagioli, *At the core of every person and every sub-personality is goodness.*

Since most of us were brought up in the religious context of original sin, this concept may be difficult to embrace. Consider the fact that most religions proclaim we were created in the image and likeness of God. This creation existed before the fall or original sin. Obviously, if we were created in the image of God, our core essence or integrity is good. We could continue in this belief that the good may be shrouded in bad, evil or sin, but the core is still good.

As a metaphor, we are like a baseball. On the outside is the horsehide cover which is the social persona or mask we show the world. If the cover is removed, we find miles of circled string tightly woven over a core. This string symbolizes the inner self, comprised of defense mechanisms, fears, doubts, good and bad, all our ways and methods of daily coping. The hard rubber core that provides the essence of the baseball, allowing it to be hit great distances, represents the God-like absolute truth, core and integrity. When we can't contact that inner self, or it can't express itself directly, it gets twisted and distorted into our sub-personalities.

The primary purpose of co-ordination is to find the basic core need of each sub-personality, bring it to conscious awareness, find acceptable and appropriate ways of expression, and satisfy and fulfill the true need. Most religions preach denial and repression of our base or negative aspects of self, and focus on shutting them out of conscious awareness, so we can be more spiritual and good. Most of our energy and thoughts, therefore, wind up dealing with the control of these negative aspects. If we are successful at this repression, these negative parts are forced underground into the unconscious and we are no longer in conscious control of our behavior.

Assagioli is one of the few who takes the opposite point of view. Instead of exhausting our energy by attempting to control the negative or evil side of self, he encourages us to find the true need, the true essence of that part of us, and embrace it. The sub-personality is acting out in rebellion and anger because it feels unappreciated, misunderstood, and unloved, much like a disowned child. Find the true need, fulfill that need, and the rebellion will cease. The function of anger is to protect us. But if the anger over-reacts and kills people, it is not meeting its true purpose, which is self-protection and self-defense. We all need the power and strength to defend ourselves when called upon. Similarly, the purpose of fear is to warn us of danger.

For example, if we are so fearful of an oncoming truck that we faint in the road, our fear did not do its proper job. The purpose of pain is to warn us of danger. If we put our hand in fire and don't feel pain, our hand will be destroyed. Pain says, "Move your hand before you hurt yourself." But if we are in twenty-four hour constant, intractable pain, it loses its value to warn.

When a sub-personality, or child, is repressed and deprived and gets nothing, it demands everything. Meet the real need, fifteen minutes of total attention, for example, and it is usually enough. Socrates said, *No one chooses to do something bad if he sees clearly that he has a choice between bad and good.* Sometimes we are blind to our options and choices.

INTEGRATION

Co-ordination deals with the development and improvement of the individual sub-personalities. Integration deals with the relationship between sub-personalities and fitting them into the person as a whole. These are often seen as pairs of opposites. The less integrated we are as individuals, the more we become one-sided and extreme in our approach to life. Dominant, angry, controlling versus submissive, passive and controlled are examples. Because of this imbalance, we tend to be drawn to our opposite, our disowned self. The conflict between us is the conflict within me. The more extreme and unbalanced we are the more we are drawn to our opposite, the missing part. The more balanced and whole we are, the more we are attracted to ourselves. This concept was discussed in Chapter Two.

These pairs of opposites must make peace with each other and see the value they all bring to the family. Using the analogy of a movie or stage play, all the actors may not be equal in their importance or roles, but each has an integral part in making this production flow in seamless perfection.

SYNTHESIS

The last phase is the culmination of individual growth. As a result of making peace within one's family of sub-personalities, we become increasingly characterized by a sense of responsibility, caring, harmonious cooperation, altruistic love and transpersonal objectives. Perfection, therefore, is the integration of the healthy self with others, with mankind, and hence the world. This idea of synthesis may sound overwhelming and idealistic, but how could you better describe what the meaning and purpose of life is all about. As we heal our outside relationships, we heal ourselves. As we heal ourselves, we heal our outside relationships. Creating a whole person is our best contribution towards world peace. As the Buddhists like to say, *One little ripple in a stream.*

Assagioli refers to levels of growth, therapy or Psychosynthesis as personal, transpersonal or spiritual. When one comes to therapy, it is usually because some part of their functioning is in distress or they find themselves in a deprived state. Therefore, the first level of therapy is to help individuals become self-actualized or fully functioning in the real world. The next step is to go on to synthesis or self-realization, terms used by both Maslow and Assagioli; a blending of self and the universe, connecting with the ultimate or God, a return to our roots or essence. Since there are two levels of growth, Assagioli refers to two selves, the 'personal self' and the 'transpersonal self'. His definition of the 'personal self' is, to perceive life without distortion or defensiveness.

Think for a moment just how difficult that is. To the extent you can achieve this, and none of us are perfect, the personality's need or tendency to self justification no longer stands in the way of clear vision. More on this in the next chapter.

SUGGESTED CHAPTER STUDY

- How did you feel in reading Assagioli's *Identification Exercise*? Years ago, in presenting this concept to college students, many of them felt stripped and vulnerable, saving "If you take away my body, my emotions, my mind, my desires, what's left?" Guess they missed the point.

- Can you see how the philosophies of Psychosynthesis can be of great value in facilitating imagery? When talking to the most vicious of sub-personalities, remember, at the core is goodness.

- For further study about Psychosynthesis, we mentioned Assagioli's books, *Act of Will* and *Psychosynthesis.* We also recommend the book *What We May Be,* by Piero Ferrucci, who was a disciple of Assagioli and his work.

CHAPTER FOURTEEN

THE OBJECTIVE OBSERVER
OR FAIR WITNESS

The many parts of us, or sub-personalities, are like actors in a play with the 'true self' being the producer/director, primarily responsible for making the entire production work. While all the actors have varying degrees of importance, even a minor player can throw things out of sync by dropping a line, missing a cue or being out of place on stage. The director's role, therefore, is to make sure the drama flows with seamless sincerity and cohesiveness.

THE DIRECTOR

Psychosynthesis refers to the role of the director as the 'personal self'. The 'personal self' is the person living in this actual world, as opposed to the 'transpersonal self', coined by both Assagioli and Maslow. The 'transpersonal self' is connected with higher conscious, the spiritual part of us that transcends the personal and connects with and blends with the universal. We will only discuss the 'personal self' here.

Think of yourself in the role of a student. As you sit in the classroom of life, your role is to listen, absorb and consider new information and how it fits into what you already know or have already learned. Therefore, we are constantly, consciously and unconsciously, accepting, modifying or rejecting everything we hear and experience. The job description of the 'personal self' is described by Assagioli as, *Two overlapping phrases; a center of 'awareness' and 'purpose', around which integration of the personality takes place, also referred to as 'consciousness' and 'will'.*

'Awareness' and 'consciousness' can be defined as one in the same, pay attention, be conscious of the world within you and around you. Listen to the words and feelings of your outside world which is constantly feeding you new, and often conflicting information. Listen to your inner world of thoughts and feelings and how they respond to this bombardment of information.

Just as 'awareness' and 'conscious' are interchangeable, so are 'purpose' and 'will'. Now that you have this new awareness or consciousness, there is a need for action. What is your purpose and do you have the will to act on and respond to the information given? Finding your own purpose in life and the will to act on this information is the way in which integration of the personality takes place. You become balanced and well functioning in the outside and inside world.

By listening and paying attention, the self becomes aware of certain truths and laws that are part of the outside world, and how they connect with inner truth and values. Processing this information leads to externalizing this reality into purpose and will, leading to direction and goals. In Psychosynthesis terms, the best job description of the 'personal self' is to become an objective observer or fair witness, who perceives life objectively, without distortion or defensiveness.

The 'personal self', therefore, is a continual dance of awareness or consciousness, which is absorbed as truth. Purpose or will is then put back into the world by way of actions and reactions according to that truth. Often the reality of awareness becomes clouded by actions and vice versa, distorting the ultimate truth of the 'personal self'. Motives become defensive, and the need to look good or be correct overrides the original awareness or factual truth; what actually happened. To that extent, the 'personal self' becomes dependent upon the external world for validation; there is a need to see reality as favorable to the self image being protected.

For example, if I need your approval to feel good about myself, I can't afford to admit to any bad motives or actions that might damage my credibility with you. However, with awareness or consciousness, truth can be perceived objectively; being a fair witness or objective observer. To the extent the status of objective observer can be achieved, the personality's need for self-justification no longer stands in the way of clear vision.

Take the scenario of a good friend saying, "You hurt me at the party last night. When you joked about my large nose and everyone laughed, you really hurt and humiliated me." How do you feel right now, listening to the words 'you hurt me'? You may feel defensive and attacked. Even if you instantly knew it was true, and you did deliberately hurt your friend last night, there is still the righteous need to protect yourself against the accusation or attack.

There are two very common defensive reactions to 'you hurt me'; denial and retaliation. If you act in denial, you will answer, "I did not." Even the kid caught with his hand in the cookie jar will cry out, "I didn't do it." When our granddaughter, Melissa, about age four, knocked over and broke a vase, she responded, "I didn't do it, my hand did it." Similarly, a husband, caught in the act of adultery in a hotel room cries out, "It isn't what you think. It's not what it looks like." What he is really saying is, "Are you going to believe me or what you see?"

The other common defense is retaliation, saying, "I had a right to do it because you hurt me even worse. You had it coming and you have no right to criticize me." But why is it necessary to deny or justify so desperately? Because hurting someone is a bad thing to do. Bad things are done by bad people. Bad people have evil characters that are socially irredeemable. Does anyone really want to admit to that? What is really being said is, "I'm not a bad person for hurting you."

The accusation 'you hurt me' and the defense of 'I'm not a bad person', are two different subjects. If that difference is understood, it is easier to deal with the problem more effectively. But we don't say, "I'm not a bad person." Instead we say, "I didn't do it." The friend's immediate need is to convince you of his pain and get you to apologize and admit you are wrong. Your need is to convince him that you are not a bad person who deliberately does bad things.

Saying 'you hurt me' is not good communication. But it is the way most people talk to each other. The proper way to express such a feeling is to say, "When you joked about my large nose at the party last night and everyone broke up laughing, I felt hurt." Can you hear the difference? Your friend's accusation of 'you hurt me' implies that you deliberately, viciously, and with malice of forethought, set out to hurt him and you were successful. It puts all of the blame and responsibility for his feelings on you and he remains innocent. Yet he hasn't disclosed his feelings at all. He didn't even really admit he was hurt. He only said "You hurt me."

In the second example, explaining why your friend felt hurt, he described your behavior and took responsibility for his own feelings. In other words, what he really said was, "As a result of the following behavior, I felt hurt." Unfortunately, saying, "I felt hurt, angry, confused, or scared," seem to be very difficult words for most people to say. Taking responsibility for one's own feelings and actions is often experienced as weak or vulnerable, even if the feeling being expressed is anger. It's easier to blame the other person. Also, admitting vulnerability is admitting how important he is to you, and that he has the power to hurt you, and even lets him know you are in a weakened condition. Being the terrible person that he is, your friend could finish you off. What he is saying is, "I'm a nice person and wouldn't take advantage of a wounded person, but the rest of the world is not as nice as I am."

By simply stating, "I felt hurt by your behavior," implies a question that could be asked directly, "What was your purpose for doing it? Was it intentional? Were you even aware of my reaction and hurt? Was it playful or vicious? I'm not judging your motives. I'm just telling you how I felt when it happened." You are now free to say whatever is true for you because you were not attacked. You could reply, "I had no idea you were sensitive about your nose. You laughed louder than anyone. I'm truly sorry." Or perhaps, "You know, I think I was mad at you and unconsciously saw a chance to get even in a public setting. That wasn't a very nice way to take care of it, I'm sorry." Why were you free to admit guilt? You weren't being attacked or accused.

Now, how does this above scenario relate to the 'personal self'? Remembering that awareness and consciousness begin with perceiving life without distortion or defensiveness, being an objective observer to reality places no blame on truth. The objective observer doesn't judge behavior or character. The objective observer merely observes, evaluates, defines, and understands.

OBSERVATION

Describe what happened. Two cars collided in the intersection. One was going thirty miles per hour from the east and one was going forty miles per hour from the north. Both drivers were injured. There is no judgment of right or wrong, just a recitation of the facts.

A husband and wife agree on a 6:00 pm dinner hour and he comes home at 6:45 pm for the fifth time in seven nights. The wife lashes out in anger at his being late and the husband yells back in defensive retaliation, saying he has no control over traffic conditions and she should be more understanding. This simple description illustrates what happened without delving into right or wrong, or taking sides.

EVALUATION

Evaluating is not the same as judging, blaming, or finding fault. It is probing deeper to ascertain the real feelings that may motivate the behavior. Is the real issue being on time or something much more complex and serious? In order to get to the deeper issues, there is a ridiculous statement you can make. It's ridiculous because it's irrelevant to your partner, but it tells you about you.

Be the wife in the above example and say, "If you loved me you would..."

- Come home on time.
- Keep your commitments.
- Do what I ask you.

- Care about my feelings and honor what's important to me.
- Want to please me.
- Want to be with me.

The obvious conclusion is, since you don't do these things, you don't love me. That conclusion is what makes it a ridiculous statement. There is probably little relationship between the husband's behavior and his love for her.

Be the husband and say, "If you loved me you would..."

- Make me more important than a silly dinner.
- Stop yelling at me.
- Try to understand I don't have total control over my time.
- Appreciate me for working hard to support us.
- Judge me for my intent and not my actual behavior.
- Stop treating me like a child.

Now the real issues are becoming apparent. By getting the husband to agree to a set dinner time, she is testing his love, loyalty, and devotion to her needs and feelings. She strongly feels if he will do this, she will feel loved. Even though the husband agrees, he feels like a child being dominated by mother and he unconsciously rebels. He may argue and say to himself, "I don't have the right to say no, but I will make sure that I'm rarely there on time, so I don't feel controlled and childlike. I can't win this war between us, but I can keep her from winning by not giving her what she wants."

DEFINING CAUSE AND EFFECT

The wife is angry that her husband is consistently late. The angrier she gets the more defensive and rebellious he gets in response. His reaction makes her even more upset, and so it goes back and forth. If a therapist could describe this cause and effect to the couple, they would probably be surprised and delighted at the new insights and revelations, and feel that the therapist was a genius. How is the therapist's information different from theirs? Simple, there is no fault, blame, or bad guy. When the wife reacted with anger, the husband rebelled as a child, making her even angrier. No implied guilt, just reactive behavior, explains why both responded the way they did.

UNDERSTANDING MOTIVE

Why do people react and rebel? A wife may say, "Because he hates me." A husband might shrug and comment, "Because she's a nag." But the truth is that most people react to protect their self image, to win in order to feel good about their power, to avoid losing and feeling bad. From all the four points above come clarification, understanding and options for better choices. When a person's ego is at stake there can be no objectivity and nothing gets resolved. An ego-centered person cannot separate behavior from ego.

What we have just presented in this chapter is a description of good communication skills in your relationships with the outside world, and their use can change your life in relating to others. But it's often difficult to incorporate these skills under the stress of life for many reasons: old habits die hard, fear of the reaction you might get, not wanting to look weak or even fear it won't work.

Start practicing these skills in guided imagery. When in a confrontation with a sub-personality, using these non-defensive reactions will almost always bring the desired result. It can be like learning a script for a play. Keep doing it until you get it right or until you get the response you want. In using this skill as the therapist, you can ask your client to become a symbol or sub-personality, and then you can speak directly to the symbol.

The client will be speaking as the symbol. In this process, you can model more appropriate responses, getting non-defensive reactions and even reconciliation with the symbol. In an imagery, whether confronting real people, such as parents, spouse or friends, or your own inner demons, the success rate for reconciliation or making peace with the other is very close to 100%. This is very supportive of what we have said previously about honoring all our sub-personalities. Listen to their criticism, don't take the remarks personally and respond without judgment.

SUGGESTED CHAPTER STUDY

- In dealing with any sub-personality within an imagery experience, be vigilant to remain the objective observer; asking questions without judgment. You are just the observer, to evaluate, to define cause and effort and most importantly, to understand motive. Especially in dealing with symbols that represent physical disease and imbalance, empathizing with their true motive can bring great insight to the client.

- Think about a hurtful comment someone made to you recently. Really analyze the comment. Using the tools of the objective observer or fair witness, did you response appropriately? If not, what would have been a better response or reaction from you?

CONCLUSION

In our guided imagery certification training, we often refer to the four levels of consciousness of the Sufi philosophy:

- Show up.
- Pay attention.
- Tell the truth.
- Don't be attached to the outcome.

Very similar wisdom is outlined by Miguel Ruiz in his book about the Toltec teachings, *The Four Agreements*. His approach is:

- Always do your best.
- Things are not always as they appear.
- Be impeccable with your word.
- Don't take anything personally.

We're also reminded of the book by Dan Millman, *The Peaceful Warrior*. In the story, a wise person asks the protagonist the following questions:

- What time is it?
- Where are you?
- Who are you?

So, let's look at this and tie it all together. 'Show up'. Similar to 'Always do your best'. In every situation, be present. In every moment, there's no past, there's no future, there's just now. Be in each separate moment so you can experience it purely for what it is now. In answering the question, 'What time is it?', don't quickly look at your watch, but simply smile and say, 'Now'. In each moment, concentrate on what's happening, pay attention to what's going on right now. Don't dilute the present with thoughts of what you need to do tomorrow or what you should have done yesterday. So, if 'What time is it?' is answered with 'Now', then 'Where are you?' is definitely just, 'Here'.

'Pay attention', be aware of all that is happening, both to you and within you, at any given moment in time. For example, if you are in an argument with someone, focus on what they are saying. Often, we're too busy preparing our rebuttal in our head to pay attention to what is actually being said. Be aware of how they are reacting. Are they angry, sad? Are they being reasonable? Similarly, in an imagery session, pay attention to your client's words and reactions. Don't be so involved in how you're going to respond, or thinking about the next question you will ask, that you miss the information being presented to you in the moment.

Turn your attention to the emotional effect that is going on within your body. Are you feeling frightened, angry, sad, vindictive, perhaps wanting to attack? To both hear and feel what the other person is saying provides empathy. Listening to and feeling your immediate response to what is being said gives you more options to react appropriately. Often when asked, "How do you feel right now?" you may reply, "I don't know." If this happens, focus on your bodily responses: perhaps sweating, feeling sick to your stomach, your head aches, your heart is pounding, or you want to run away or even attack. Let your body tell you what's going on and you'll know what you're feeling. With this clear focus, you can appreciate what's happening, separate past prejudice and judgment and see that 'Things may not always be as they appear'. Removing the negativity of the collective consciousness, you can perhaps see love or compassion in a situation, whereas before you just saw pain or disgust.

'Tell the truth' and 'Be impeccable with your words' are straightforward enough. This is about telling your own truth, the truth according to your own authenticity. Not clouded by what you think someone wants you to say or by what you think someone wants to hear. It's about your own truth, according to you.

The truth in the moment is what's going on right now, between you and your environment, or perhaps between you and your client. Your truth involves what the other is saying to you and how your body is responding to what you are hearing. Only then can you respond. You might say something like, *"I feel attacked right now and find it very difficult to listen to your words. Part of me wants to attack in return, but I really care about you and appreciate your honesty and anger. I don't want to be defensive. I want to work this out."* This is the kind of truth both the Toltec and Sufi philosophies are referring to. In an imagery, can you see how these words could sooth even the most vicious sub-personality?

'Don't be attached to the outcome'. You might say, *"Of course, I'm attached to the outcome. I showed up, I paid attention, told my truth and now I'm expecting a certain result."* If you follow these steps, the outcome was given over to the Universe. You have no control of what happens. You know you did your best, so now, it's just about stepping back and watching what happens. Whatever happens is ok.

When you attach to a particular outcome, you are putting all your energy into how you think it should unfold. And sometimes, the Universe has bigger and better plans. Face it, you have no control over other people's responses. You may be a very intimidating and controlling person who prides yourself on getting what you want, but that is only a temporary situation, not an outcome. When you attach to an outcome, you are literally defining your identity and worth on how a certain situation unfolds or how someone responds to you. If a person doesn't like you, does that make you a bad person? Of course not. Being attached is giving away your power to other people or to the success or failure of a particular event or situation. Your self-worth becomes no better than a particular outcome or reaction. You then become powerless.

'Show up', 'Pay attention', and 'Tell the truth', which all include separating from the beliefs of others, allow you to not be attached to the outcome. You've done your best, and that's all you are responsible for. And then, the other person has personal responsibility for how they feel and respond to you. And indeed, what other people think is truly none of your business. Don't take anything personally. Reminds us of a wonderful book years ago by Terry Cole Whittaker, *What You Think of Me is None of My Business.*

Connecting with any outcome or person is respecting what happens as just information, and perhaps giving you lessons for personal growth. Doing a bad job in a presentation at work, or feeling the session with your client didn't go well, doesn't mean you're a bad person or a bad therapist. But the response or outcome could bring important information for improving and growing. Attaching is truly giving your power away to others to define you, whereas connecting affords the respect of any outcome to bring clarity and avenues to change or, for that matter, not change.

In many Native American cultures, one of their rituals includes the sacred circle; people standing to form a circle. Take a minute to see that in your mind. Did you see a group of people in that circle holding hands? That's attaching. Holding hands creates one entity; your individual identity is lost in the circle. But, in this ritual, each extends their arms out, left palm up, right palm down, the right hand inches above the other's left hand, but they don't touch. Subtle, but the flow of energy from one to the other, each person as an individual, separate and unique, but yet part of something greater; the circle. That's being connected. Drawing from others without defining themselves by the circle, allowing the energy to flow through them, is not being attached to the outcome.

'Show up', 'Pay attention', 'Tell your truth', and 'Don't be attached to the outcome', we can say, *'The time is now'.* 'Where are you?' can be answered with *'Right here'.* This brings the answer to Millman's last question, 'Who are you?'. With your full authenticity and joy, we invite you to say, *'The best I can be in this moment'.* This is great wisdom to integrate into your personal life, as well as in your work as a Guided Imagery Therapist.

We've provided you with structure and tools to use in facilitating this powerful modality, and your job, as therapist, should first and foremost include:

- Show up. Be present and provide a safe place for your client.
- Pay attention. Listen to your client with no judgment or prejudice. You're just gathering information.
- Tell the truth. Be authentic and be aware of what's going on between you and your client. That connection is vital.
- Don't be attached to the outcome. Even though you may have a goal in mind as to where an imagery should go, always follow the client. It's their journey.

In closing, we hope you have enjoyed our words and that the concepts presented will help you in refining your skills. On an altruistic level, as we all work with guided imagery and make peace with the various parts of self, we can pay it forward to our relationships, our community, our country, and ultimately the world. *Let there be peace on earth and let it begin with me.*

Namaste,
Chuck and Patti Leviton

AFTERWORD

We have presented you tools and information that should add greatly to your skills in understanding, creating and benefiting from the power of guided imagery, both for yourself and your clients. We sincerely hope this has empowered you. But know there is no substitute for the intimate, face-to-face experience of imagery to truly appreciate the process. If you would like to experience one of our weekend seminars, or our complete certification program here in our offices in Palm Springs, California, or the many cities across the country that might be near you, check out our website at www.synergyseminars.com for a complete schedule of events. Or perhaps, if you would be interested, we could bring this program to your city or facility. We would be happy to discuss this with you. We have a passion for the process and love sharing it with others.

Synergy Seminars
441 South Calle Encilia – Suite 17
Palm Springs, CA 92262
760-322-5200 or toll free 888.791.6329

ABOUT THE AUTHORS

 Charles D. Leviton, EdD recently retired from being a full-time professor at Orange Coast College, Costa Mesa, California, where he taught 'Introduction to Guided Imagery' and 'Marriage and Family Life'. A licensed Marriage and Family Therapist and certified hypnotherapist, Leviton has been successfully using imagery for over 40 years in his teaching and private practice. He is past president and current board member of the American Association for the Study of Mental Imagery and is also a diplomat of the American Psychotherapy Association.

 Patti Leviton, MA has 25 years experience with Guided Imagery. A former stockbroker, Patti had a miraculous healing from cancer over 25 years ago, and now devotes herself full-time as a certified hypnotherapist and Guided Imagery Therapist. Facilitating numerous cancer groups and women's groups, she has created more than 30 different guided imagery CDs. She is a former board member of the American Holistic Health Association and author of the book, *The Miracle of Words.*

Together, the Levitons provide a full certification program to train both professionals and laypersons to become Guided Imagery Therapists. Their offices are in Palm Springs, CA, and they devote their full energies to traveling the country doing their seminars. This is their third book together. They have also written, *The Conflict Between Us is the Conflict Within Me*, a book about using imagery as a tool in achieving healthy relationships, as well as *Inner Peace – Outward Power*, a book and 2-CD set to use with any 12 step program to recovery.

BIBLIOGRAPHY

CHAPTER ONE: HISTORY OF GUIDED IMAGERY

Benson, Herbert, *Timeless Healing*, Simon and Schuster, 1996.

Dossey, Larry, *Healing Words*, Harpers San Francisco, 1993.

Lipton, Bruce and Bhaerman, Steve, *Spontaneous Evolution*, Hay House, 2009.

Moyers, Bill, *Healing and the Mind*, video recordings, David Grubin Productions, 1993.

Naparstek, Belleruth, *Staying Well with Guided Imagery*, Hachette Book Group, 1994.

Pert, Candace, *Molecules of Emotion*, Simon and Schuster, 1997.

Walter, Jakob, *The Diary of a Napoleonic Foot Soldier*, Penguin Books, 1991.

CHAPTER TWO: WHAT IS GUIDED IMAGERY

Achterberg, Jeanne, *Imagery in Healing*, Shambhala, 1984.

Allport, Gordon, *Man's Search for Meaning*, Beacon Press, 2000.

Jung, Carl, *Man and his Symbols*, Dell Publishing, 1964.

Leuner, Hanscarl, *Guided Affective Imagery*, Thieme-Straiton, Inc., 1984.

Leviton, Charles and Patti, *The Conflict Between Us is the Conflict Within Me*, Brown Publishing, 2002.

Myss, Caroline, *Anatomy of the Spirit*, Random House, 1996.

Myss, Caroline, *Why People Don't Heal and How They Can*, Random House, 1997.

CHAPTER THREE: FIRST THINGS FIRST – THE INDUCTION

Campbell, Don, *The Mozart Effect,* Avon Books, 1997.

Pert, Candace, *Molecules of Emotion*, Simon and Schuster, 1997.

Pert, Candace, *Your Body is Your Subconscious Mind*, audio series, Sounds True, 2000.

Provost, Mark, *Audio Music*, Solara Recording and Production, www.musicforguidedimagery.com, 2006.

Reznick, Charlotte, *The Power of Your Child's Imagination*, Perigee Book, 2009.

CHAPTER FOUR: WHY INTRA PERSONAL IMAGERY

Lerner, Harriet, *The Dance of Deception*, Harper-Collins, 1989.

Stauffer, Edith, *Unconditional Love and Forgiveness*, Triangle Publishers, 1987.

CHAPTER FIVE: THE WORK OF THE PIONEERS

Campbell, Joseph, *Hero with a Thousand Faces*, New World Library, 1991.

Campbell, Joseph*, Myths to Live By*, Viking Press, 1972.

Desoille, Robert, *The Directed Daydream*, a series of three lectures at the Sorbonne University, Paris, France, January 1965.

Donn, Linda, *Freud and Jung – Years of Friendship, Years of Loss*, Collier Books, 1988.

Freud, Sigmund, *The Interpretation of Dreams*, Avon Books, 1980.

Jung, Carl, *Man and his Symbols,* Dell Publishing, 1964.

Jung, Carl, *The Red Book*, W. W. Norton, 2009.

Leuner, Hanscarl, *Guided Affective Imagery*, Thieme-Straiton, Inc., 1984.

Miller, Emmett, *Deep Healing*, Hay House, 1997.

Naparstek, Belleruth, *Staying Well with Guided Imagery*, Hachette Book Group, 1994.

Naparstek, Belleruth, *Invisible Heroes – Survivors of Trauma and How They Heal*, Bantam Books, 2004.

Roth, Michael, *Freud*, Alfred A. Knopf, 1998.

Simonton, O. Carl, *Getting Well Again*, Bantam Books, 1992.

CHAPTER SIX: CHOOSING A SUBJECT – THE PRESENTING PROBLEM

Andrews, Ted, *Animal-Speaks,* Llewellyn Publications, 1993.

Andrews, Ted, *Animal-Wise,* Dragonhawk Publishing, 1997.

Hay, Louise, *You Can Heal Your Life*, Hay House, 1993.

Truman, Karol, *Feelings Buried Alive Never Die*, Olympus Distributing, 1993.

CHAPTER SEVEN: WHERE TO BEGIN THE IMAGERY

Braden, Gregg, *The God Code*, Hay House, 2004.

Naparstek, Belleruth, *Invisible Heroes – Survivors of Trauma and How They Heal*, Bantam Books, 2004.

Reznick, Charlotte, *The Power of Your Child's Imagination*, Perigee Book, 2009.

CHAPTER EIGHT: STRUCTURE – THE GOALS AND INTENT

Jung, Carl, *Dreams*, Princeton University Press, 1974.

Jung, Carl, *Man and his Symbols*. Dell Publishing, 1964.

Jung, Carl, *The Red Book*, W. W. Norton, 2009.

Leviton, Charles and Patti, *Inner Peace – Outward Power, Guided Imagery to Use with the 12 Steps to Recovery*, Aardvark Global Publishing, 2007.

CHAPTER NINE: A WORD ABOUT BELIEF SYSTEMS

Bradshaw, John, *Homecoming: Reclaiming and Championing Your Inner Child*, Bantam Books, 1990.

Bradshaw, John, *Family Secrets – What You Don't Know Can Hurt You,* Bantam Books, 1995.
Myss, Caroline, *Anatomy of the Spirit*, Random House, 1996.
Myss, Caroline, *Why People Don't Heal and How They Can*, Random House, 1997.

CHAPTER TEN: KEEPING THE IMAGERY MOVING WITHOUT CONTROLING THE OUTCOME

Naparstek, Belleruth*, Invisible Heroes – Survivors of Trauma and How They Heal*, Bantam Books, 2004.
Pert, Candace, *Your Body is Your Subconscious Mind*, audio series, Sounds True, 2000.
Rodgers, Carl, *Client-Centered Therapy,* Houghton Mifflin, 1951.
Truman, Karol, *Feelings Buried Alive Never Die*, Olympus Distributing, 1993.
Wolf, Fred Alan, *Taking the Quantum Leap*, Harper & Row, 1989.

CHAPTER ELEVEN: EXTRA TOOLS

Benson, Herbert, *Timeless Healing*, Simon and Schuster, 1996.
Silva, Jose, *The Silva Mind Control Method*, Penguin Books, 1977.
Shorr, Joseph, *Go See the Movie in Your Head*, Ross-Erickson, 1983.

CHAPTER THIRTEEN: PSYCHOSYNTHESIS

Assagioli, Roberto, *Act of Will*, Arkana, 1993.
Assagioli, Roberto*, Psychosyntheisis,* Arkana, 1993.
Braden, Gregg, *Fractal Time*, Hay House, 2009.
Braden, Gregg, *The Spontaneous Healing of Belief*, Hay House, 2008.
Ferrucci, Piero, *What We May Be*, Jeremy P. Tarcher, 1982.
Fromm, Eric, *The Art of Loving,* Ross-Erickson, 1983.
Lipton, Bruce and Bhaerman, Steve, *Spontaneous Evolution*, Hay House, 2009.
Lipton, Bruce, *The Biology of Belief*, Mountain of Love/Elite Books, 2005.
Maslow, Abraham, *Toward a Psychology of Being*, Van Nostrand, Reinhold, 1968.

May, Rollo, *Man's Search for Himself,* W. W. Norton, 1955.
Pert, Candace, *Molecules of Emotion*, Simon and Schuster, 1997.
Pert, Candace, *Your Body is Your Subconscious Mind*, audio series, Sounds True, 2000.
Stone, Hal and Sidra, *Embracing Ourselves,* Nataraj Publishing, 1989.

CHAPTER FOURTEEN: THE OBJECTIVE OBSERVER OR FAIR WITNESS

Assagioli, Roberto, *Act of Will,* Arkana, 1993.
Assagioli, Roberto, *Psychoyntheisis,* Arkana, 1993.
Ferrucci, Piero, *What We May Be*, Jeremy P. Tarcher, 1982.

CONCLUSION

Millman, Dan, *The Way of the Peaceful Warrior*, H. J. Kramer, 1984.
Ruiz, Don Miguel, *The Four Agreements,* Amber-Allen, 2000.
Whittaker, Terry Cole, *What You Think of Me is None of My Business,* Jove Publications, 1991.

APPENDIX

BODY IN COLOR
INDUCTION

Take a deep breath, slowly breathing in through your nose, exhaling
   out your mouth, and again.
With every breath, feel your body relax.
With every breath feel a sense of peace and calm.
Nothing you have to do, nothing you have to say, but just relax.
Right now, in your imagination, I invite you to see, feel and sense
   the base of your spine.
As if this is the very center of your body right now.
And from this place, see, feel, sense the color red filling every part
   of you.
Radiating down your legs, your arms your whole body filled in this
   beautiful red.
Now watch, as that red slowly starts to change.
Swirling, churning, dancing into orange.
Can you see it?
The most exquisite orange, vibrant, pulsating through every organ,
   every gland in your body.
And your focus is drawn to your belly.
Orange, brightening now, lightening now to yellow.

Even with your eyes closed you can almost see the room getting
   lighter.
Brighter as your whole body fills with this exquisite yellow sunlight,
   sunshine.
And your focus is drawn to your solar plexus.
That place right below your ribcage.
You can actually feel this yellow as now it deepens to a beautiful
   green.
The most breathtaking green you've ever seen.
And your focus is drawn to your heart.
Listen, you can actually hear your heart beat right now.
Pulsating through every vein, every artery in your body the color
   green.
Green now changing to blue.
A peaceful, blue, a color of calm.
Every part of you now is bathed in this beautiful color.
A wash of peace and your focus is drawn to your throat.
Literally, swallow in this blue filling every part of you in peace and
   calm.
Blue changing now to purple.
Iridescent, opalescent, this purple almost moves through your body.
You've never seen such a marvelous color.
And you're aware that your attention is drawn to the middle of your
   forehead.
Purple changing one last time to white.
Your focus is drawn to the very top of your head.
The most beautiful white light cascading down your whole body.
Bathed, caressed in this beautiful white light.
You feel so peaceful, so relaxed, ready now to begin a journey...

WHITE LIGHT
INDUCTION

This is your time to relax.
I invite you right now to close your eyes.
Take a deep breath.
Breathing in through your nose and out through your mouth.

And again, you can feel your body begin to relax.
In your imagination you see a beautiful light shining right above
   your head.
Can you see it?
You can actually feel your scalp tingle.
This light begins to move down and is shining in your face.
Even with your eyes closed, you can see this light.
Relaxing all the muscles in your face.
The tiny muscles around your eyes relaxing.
Your cheeks relaxing, your lips soft and supple.
This light is now shining on your shoulders.
And you can literally feel any tension just melting away.
Down your arms, your wrists, your hands.
This light filling each of your fingers.
Your hands are actually tingling now.
This light is shining down your back, your chest, your belly, your hips.
Every organ, every gland bathed in this light.
Down your legs, your thighs, your knees, so relaxed.
Your shins, down your ankles and into your feet.
Your feet filled in this beautiful light.
Every part of you aglow.
So relaxed, so peaceful.
Right now, I invite you to be in your place of peace
It can be at the beach, in a meadow, in the desert.
Allow your imagination to take you to that place.
A place perhaps you have been before and enjoyed.
Or somewhere you've read about or seen pictures of.
Just be there.
A place where you feel peaceful and safe.
Enjoy the moment and drink in the beauty of this marvelous spot
   in your mind's eye.
Listen to the sounds.
Smell the marvelous aromas.
Feel the temperature of the air on your skin.
You can even taste it.
If you're at the beach, perhaps a faint salt water on your lips.
Or the sweet taste of pollen on your palette.

Experience with all your senses.
I'll give you some time to relish the moment.
Ready to begin our adventure together...

PLACE OF PEACE
INDUCTION

Right now just close your eyes.
Take a deep breath.
Slowly breathing in through your nose and out through your month.
And again.
You can feel your body begin to relax.
For the next ten or fifteen minutes, I will be taking you on a journey.
A journey in your imagination.
Now, there's no right way or wrong way to do this.
So just allow yourself to relax and watch what happens.
I invite you right now, in your imagination, to be in a beautiful open meadow.
The day is perfect.
The splendor of green grass and flowers.
Lift your head up and see the sun gently shining down on your face.
The temperature of the air is just right, not too hot, not too cool, just right.
The sky is so blue, lazy clouds floating above.
It's breathtaking.
Perhaps you can even feel a gentle breeze on your face.
Look around, drink in the beauty of this spot.
I'll give you a few moments to just enjoy yourself.
You feel so peaceful and safe.
All the time in the world to just be in this meadow.
Breathe in the pristine fresh air.
Perhaps you can even smell the sweet aromas of the wild flowers.
Listen, what do you hear?
Perhaps the scampering of small animals, or the birds.
You hear the sounds of water.

You notice that up ahead is a small, beautiful lake.
Do you see it?
Your step quickens a bit as you walk towards this peaceful lagoon.
So calm, the reflection off the water is like a mirror.
A reflection of all the trees and the magnificence of this meadow.
How do you feel just being here?
So peaceful, so relaxed.
Ready to begin our adventure together...

PARADOXICAL INTENTION INDUCTION

The following induction was originally written as an imagery script for use with teens suffering with anxiety and stress. You can see how this induction could be modified for anyone who is really tense, with difficulty in relaxing. Paradoxical intention is designed for the client to experience even more tension. And then, since the body cannot hold tension forever, given permission to release and let go, will bring some marvelous results. This induction could, by itself, be a great experience to relieve stress and anxiety.

Find a comfortable place to sit down or lie down and just relax
This is your time.
No distractions.
Nobody telling you what to do, no teachers, no parents.
In your imagination, I'll be taking you on an adventure.
So just allow whatever comes to mind.
Whether you see it like watching a movie, or just feel or sense it.
There's really no right way or wrong way to do this.
So, just close your eyes and let's begin.
Take a deep breath and slowly exhale.
Literally feel your body begin to relax.
Take another deep breath.
Slowly breathing in through your nose and out through your mouth.
And again.
Right now, focus all your attention on the base of your spine.
Literally tighten up your butt.

Come on, tighten up.
Feel the tensing, tighter, tighter.
Suck it in.
Hold it.
Now, let it go.
And as you let go, see the color red.
Like a cloud filling your whole body.
Down your legs, your arms, even your face.
Filled in red.
Now watch as this red slowly changes to orange.
Can you see it?
Bright, the most beautiful orange you've ever seen.
And you begin to think about your belly.
Literally start to tense your belly, tighter, tighter.
Hold it.
Now let it go.
Relax.
And in that relaxation see the color orange.
Filling every bit of you, down to your fingers, your toes.
Every part of you in orange.
Now, you're thinking about your lungs.
Take in a deep breath.
Come on, take a deep breath, and hold it.
Sucking in your breath, tighter, tighter.
Really hold your breath.
Excellent.
Now, let it go.
And as you take a deep breath, you see the color yellow.
Filling your whole body.
Your arms, your legs, your back, your butt, your chest.
Your belly, every part of you in yellow.
Moving now to your shoulders.
Arch your shoulders.
Tensing, tighter, tighter.
Your shoulders are up to your ears.
Hold it.
Excellent.

And now let them drop.
Feel your shoulders relax.
And you see the color green.
Filling every part of you.
The color is changing one more time.
Now it's blue.
It's beautiful.
Can you see this blue?
And you are aware of your throat.
Right now, swallow.
And tense your jaw, clenching your teeth.
Tighter, tighter.
Good.
Now, let it go.
Let your jaw just drop.
And watch as this color blue fills you.
Watch this blue almost like a cloud filling every part of your body.
Blue dancing now into purple.
See it?
The color is filling your whole face.
Right now, squeeze and tense up your eyes, tighter now.
Make a silly face.
Hold it.
Excellent.
Now, let it go.
And as you relax watch this purple filling your body.
A wave of color.
Every cell, every molecule, every organ, every gland.
Filled in this beautiful purple.
The color now changes one last time.
To silvery, sparkly white.
Literally feel this light shining down on the top of your head.
Your scalp is tingling, your hair is tingling.
This beautiful light down your face, down your shoulders.
Your arms, your legs, your whole body.
Filled in this white light.
Ready now to being our journey together...

That's the end of the induction, but below is how we finished the actual imagery script, incorporating the use of the alpha trigger. We hope this will give you some ideas to create your own adventures for healing and relaxation, and relieving stress for your clients.

So, right now, being so relaxed.
In your imaginations, you find yourself in a beautiful place in nature.
Oh, this is your special place.
It could be in a meadow.
Or on the beach, by the ocean or a lake.
Maybe a place you've read about in a book.
It's your special place.
So peaceful.
It's beautiful.
I'll give you some time to find your special spot and just look around.
Enjoy yourself.
Now, nobody's around.
You feel so safe and relaxed.
All the time in the world to enjoy your special place.
Where are you?
You begin to look around.
As you're exploring, you notice a present sitting on the ground.
See it?
It's a gift just for you.
Just sitting there.
You bend down and pick it up.
Open it.
It's something you've always wanted.
It's perfect.
A present just for you.
And you smile.
Come on, smile.
This is your special place where you're so relaxed.
And no one is around to bug you.
And there's a gift just for you.
Knowing that whenever you smile,

During the day, at school, at home,
You can return to this place whenever you want to relax.
You smile.
Come one, smile.
And slowly, it's time to come back to this room.
Remembering everything you just experienced.
How relaxed your body feels.
Remembering your special place.
And most important, remembering the gift that will always be there
    just for you.
Take a deep breath.
Wiggle your toes.
Wiggle your fingers, and smile.
And when you're ready, you can open your eyes.
Welcome back, welcome back. And smile.

THE HOUSE
IMAGERY EXPERIENCE

Below is the script for our favorite imagery, 'The House'. The experience is rich with symbolism. This is usually the first imagery experience we do with new clients. When you read this imagery, make sure you allow sufficient time for the client to experience every suggestion. Read it slowly and add pauses. Assure the listener that there is no right way, or wrong way to do imagery. Just allow the imagination to unfold a story in their head. Whatever happens is fine.

The experience suggests seeing a house, which symbolically tends to represent self; how we see ourselves in our lives right now. Therefore, each room represents a different part or aspect of self. The living room usually means how we receive or connect with others and how we wish to be viewed in the world. The dining room tends to mean how we nurture others, and so on. Following the script, a full listing is provided for all the rooms and their meanings. Of course, during the imagery, don't interpret the symbols; leave that for after the experience. As the adventure unfolds and the whole house has been explored, the client is invited to go to the attic, which tends to represent the past and perhaps any unfinished business, and find something that draws their attention and bring it downstairs. Where they wish to place it, be it the living room, kitchen, wherever, can be a powerful tool in allowing the subconscious to provide information on past events or traumas that need to be healed or past experiences that can empower. Any ambient music in the background can add to the effectiveness. Allow time after the imagery to discuss what the client experienced, and look at the symbolism, and possible interpretations. Have fun and remember, slow down in your delivery, take your time and enjoy. The dialogue after the experience can be amazing.

Right now, I invite you to close your eyes.
Take a deep breath.
Breathing in through your nose and out through your mouth.
And again.
With each breath, feel your body start to unwind.
All tension and stress just melting away.
You can feel your body relax as we start this journey together.
So, let us begin.
In your imagination, I invite you to be in a place of peace.
It could be a place where you've been before.
Or maybe a place that you've read about.
Or maybe, an imaginary spot.
But, just be there right now.
A place where you feel relaxed and safe.
A place in nature. Are you there? Just be there.
With all your senses experience this place.
Look around. What do you see?
Drink in the beauty of this marvelous spot.
You're all alone, but you feel peaceful and content.
Listen, what are the sounds?
Truly hear all the wonderful sounds around you.
Perhaps leaves rustling in the trees.
Or the sounds of water from a small brook.
Be still and just listen.

Perhaps the scampering of small animals or birds above.
What's the temperature of the air on your skin?
It's just right for you.
There could even be a gentle breeze blowing on your face.
You can even taste this place. Lick your lips.
Perhaps sweet pollen from flowers.
Or even the taste of salt water if you're by an ocean.
And now, take a deep breath.
Smell the sweet aromas in the air.
What are all the wonderful smells you're experiencing right now?
With all your senses, truly be in this place, your place of peace.
All the time in the world, leisurely start walking along.
Drinking in the beauty, the peace.
You can actually feel your body relax even more as you begin to
    stroll along.
A path opens up and it's a marvelous day to explore this spot.
I'll give you some time to just enjoy yourself.
As you're walking along, you notice a house in the distance.
Do you see it?
It intrigues you and your step quickens.
You find yourself standing in front of this house.
What is your impression?
How do you feel about this house?
What do you like most about this house, what do you like least?
Slowly, you find yourself walking up to the front door and you knock.
The door gently opens.
You're greeted by someone, inviting you into the house.
Who is this person?
How do you feel about entering this house?
What do you feel about this person?
It takes a moment for your eyes to adjust to the inside light.
You find yourself in the living room of this house.
Look around. What do you see?
Drink in all the details of this room.
What do you like most, what do you like least?
You now leave the living room and find your way into the dining room.
Again, look around. What do you see?

How do you feel in this room?
What details catch your eye in this room?
What do you like most about this room?
What do you like least?
You wend your way, now, into the kitchen.
What does this room look like? Is it modern, old fashioned?
You explore, open the refrigerator, what's inside?
You look in the pantry.
With all your senses, pay attention to all the details in the kitchen.
What do you like most, and least.
You find yourself now going into the bedroom.
Really look around.
Look at the bed, does it look comfortable?
Could you see yourself taking a nap.
Or perhaps even making love on that bed?
How do you feel in this room?
What do you like most and what do you like least?
Heading now into the bathroom, what do you see here?
It is clean, modern or perhaps old fashioned?
Pay attention to all the details.
There's a mirror on the wall, see it?
Go over and look into the mirror.
What do you see?
What is the reflection looking back at you?
What about this room do you like the most?
And what do you like least?
Now, go up to the attic.
Climbing the stairs, it's a little dark and dusty.
And it takes a little while for your eyes to adjust to the dim light.
What do you see up there? I'll give you some time to explore.
Now there's something here, in the attic.
An item that is drawing your attention.
Look around, what is it?
And you find yourself bringing this item downstairs.
I'll give you some time to decide where you would like to put it.
You just know there's a special place for it, a place it needs to be.
That being completed, it's time to leave the house.

You find yourself going back through the house and to the front door.

And you leave.

Walking out of the house you stop.

Turn around and look once again at this house.

What are your feelings right now?

And I'll give you some time right now to change anything you would like about this house.

Anything.

You can change anything.

Or perhaps you like it just the way it is.

I'll give you some time.

Perhaps moving its location.

Or changing a color in a room or even adding a window or two.

You can do anything you wish.

And, now, slowly you walk away from the house.

Remembering everything.

Remember the person that greeted you.

Remembering the living room, the dining room, the kitchen.

Remembering your impressions of the bedroom and bathroom.

The attic and also what was the item you brought downstairs.

Where you placed it.

Remembering it all, it's time to start your journey back to this room.

Slowly, wiggle your toes, wiggle your fingers.

Take a deep breath and as you exhale, make a sound, a real sound.

Coming back into this room awake, alive and refreshed.

And when you're ready, you can open your eyes.

Welcome back.

THE VARIOUS ROOMS IN THE HOUSE TEND TO REPRESENT:

Allowing the imagination to see, feel and sense whatever unfolds can be a powerful tool in discovering insights into ourselves and our world. Similar to a dream, we can interpret what the experiences and symbols may mean.

The House – how we view ourselves in the world

Living room – how we wish to be seen in the world

Dining room – how we nurture other people

Kitchen – how we nurture ourselves or how we were nurtured as a child

Bedroom – our sensuality and sexuality, our creativity

Bathroom – our pride in our physical appearance and general maintenance of our body

Attic – memories from our past or what is it from our past that needs resolution or attention

POSSIBLE ITEMS FOUND IN THE ATTIC:

Necklace – according to Carl Jung, it symbolizes belonging to a tribe

Pin – it symbolizes the belonging to self; confidence, self-love, self-esteem

Ring – symbol of a union between two people, or a union within self

Bracelet – sacred symbol of believing in a cause, knowing your truth

White light – surrounding by the protection of your creator

Empty box – a powerful symbol of all there is, full potential of anything you want and need, pure abundance, true confidence and self-esteem

Sword – symbol of masculine energy

Vase – symbol of feminine energy

Book – symbol of wisdom and history

Picture or picture album – symbol of our ancestors, our heritage, our tribe

Robe or garment – symbol of being honored

Watch or clock – symbol of divine timing, to begin an adventure

Purse or bag – lessons learned

Money or coins – symbol of prosperity

Musical instrument – speaking your truth and being understood

SYMPTOMS AS METAPHOR
A DIRECTORY OF SYMBOLS

ANIMALS

Antelope – speed and adaptability of the mind
Armadillo – personal protection, discrimination and empathy
Ass – wisdom and humility
Badger – bold self-expression and reliance, keeper of stories
Bat – transition and initiation
Bear – awakening the power of the unconscious
Beaver – the building of dreams
Bison or buffalo – manifesting abundance through right action
Bobcat – silence and secrets
Bull – fertility
Cat – mystery, magic and independence
Cougar – coming into your own power
Coyote – wisdom and folly
Deer – gentleness and innocence, gentle luring to new adventures
Dogs – faithfulness and protection
Dolphin – the power of breath and sound
Elephant – ancient power, strength and royalty, sacred ritual of grieving

Elk – strength and nobility
Fox – feminine magic of camouflage, shape shifting and invisibility
Giraffe – farsightedness
Goat – surefootedness and seeking new heights
Groundhog – mystery of death without dying, trance, dreams
Horse – travel, power and freedom
Leopard – overcoming our demons and dragons, renewal of vision and vitality
Lion – assertion of the feminine and the power of the female sun
Lynx – secrets and vision of the hidden and unseen
Moose – primal feminine energies and the magic of life and death
Mouse – attention to detail
Opossum – the use of appearances
Otter – joy, playfulness and sharing
Panther – reclaiming one's true power
Porcupine – renewed sense of wonder
Prairie dog – sense of community
Rabbit – fertility and new life
Raccoon – dexterity and disguise
Ram – seeking new beginnings
Rat – success, restlessness and shrewdness
Rhinoceros – ancient wisdom
Sea lions and seals – active imagination, creativity and lucid dreaming
Skunk – sensuality, respect and self-esteem
Squirrel – activity and preparedness
Tiger – passion, power, devotion and sensuality
Weasel – sly and secret circumvention and/or pursuit
Whale – creation, power of song, awakening inner depths
Wolf – guardianship, ritual, loyalty and spirit

BIRDS

Black bird – understanding of the energies of mother nature
Blue bird – modesty, unassuming confidence and happiness
Blue jay – the proper use of power
Canary – power of song and voice
Cardinal – renewed vitality through recognizing self-importance

Chicken – fertility and sacrifice

Cock – sexuality, watchfulness and resurrection crane, longevity and creation through focus

Crow – the secret magic of creation is calling

Doves – feminine energies of peace, maternity and prophecy

Ducks – emotional comfort and protection

Eagles – illumination of spirit, healing and creation

Goose – the call of the quest and travels to legendary places

Gull – responsible behavior and communication

Hawk – visionary power and guardianship

Heron – aggressive self-determination and self-reliance

Hummingbird – tireless joy and the nectar of life

Mockingbird – finding your sacred song and recognition of your innate abilities

Ostrich – becoming grounded

Owl – the mystery of magic, omens, silent wisdom and vision in the night

Parrot – sunshine and color healing

Peacock – resurrection and wise vision

Pelican – renewed buoyancy and unselfishness

Penguin – lucid dreaming and astral projection

Pheasant – family fertility and sexuality

Pigeon – return to the love and security of home

Raven – magic, shape shifting and creation

Road runner – mental speed and agility

Robin – spread of new growth

Sparrow – awakening and triumph of common nobility

Stork – birth and unspoken communication

Swallow – protection, warmth for home and proper perspective

Swans – awakening the true beauty and power of the self

Turkey – shared blessings and harvest

Vulture – purification, death and rebirth, new vision

Woodpecker – the power of rhythm and discrimination

BODY

Ankles – the ability to make decisions

Arms – our ability to connect with this world

Back – our courage, belief systems and ethics
Chest – our physical strength
Ears – ability to hear clearly
Eye – ability to see clearly
Feet – our basic safety in the world, our community
Fingers – paying attention to all the details of life
Hair – our connection to the divine, our spiritual connection or strength
Hands – our ability to be connected to another person
Heart – our space of love and healing
Hips – our balance and sense of security in the world
Knees – ability to be flexible, not be stubborn
Neck – the ability to see different perspectives
Nose – ability to smell and primal feelings
Sexual organs – our creativity
Shins – the minor irritations of life
Shoulders – the place of carrying our past
Stomach – place of holding pain and need for forgiveness
Teeth – ability to analyze and process a situation or problem
Thighs – our basic morals and judgment
Throat – speaking our truth
Thymus – knowing our truth and authenticity

CHAKRAS

Base of spine – grounding and connection to tribe, safety and security
Belly – creativity, sensuality and sexuality
Solar Plexis – self-esteem and confidence
Heart – physical healing and connection to others
Thymus – knowing our own truth
Throat – speaking our own truth, and also peace and calm
Forehead – mystical third eye to see the world behind our eyes
Top of head – crown chakra of connection with our spirituality and creation

COLORS

Black – an inward journey of connecting with self
Blue – peace and calm (depression)
Bronze – stronger connection to creation and art
Brown – grounding and safety
Copper – healing power of the physical body
Gold – higher connection to the material world
Gray – all colors combined in perfect balance and harmony and understanding
Green – healing and growth (envy)
Orange – creativity (stubborn)
Purple – spirituality and wisdom (vanity)
Red – passion (anger)
Silver – higher connection to the spiritual world
White – an outward journey of connecting with the world
Yellow – energy and life (fear)

CRYSTALS

Alexandrite – stimulates psychic gifts and opens up the higher center of awareness
Amber – feminine power, helps women find their internal empowerment
Amethyst – spiritual clarity and love of the higher mind
Aquamarine – balanced emotions and a deep commitment to sharing one's true feelings
Blue-agate – anchor our spirit in our body, preserving physical energy
Bloodstone – ability to purify the blood
Citrine – transition and new beginnings
Cornelian – promote health and well-being
Diamond – stands for fidelity, loyalty and divine love
Hematite – magnetic qualities for grounding the spirit
Lapis lazuli – represents the wisdom principle of the higher mind
Onyx – stimulate healing by magnetizing the blood
Peridot – stimulates confidence and love of self
Rose quartz – stands for love
Ruby – essence of vitality and the regenerative forces

Sapphire – fidelity in relationships, clarity of thought and a decisive
mind

Tanzanite – healing and a commitment to expressing truth and
wisdom and love

Tiger's eye – brings prosperity and abundance

Topaz – source of courage

Turquoise – contains the spirit of the creator and a commitment of
telling the truth

DIRECTIONS

Right side – coming from logical, masculine, analytical thinking, or
about the future

Left side – coming from emotional, feminine energy, or about the
past

From above – spiritual and mystical

From below – grounded and centered

West – the past and lessons learned

East – the future and dreams and goals

North – masculine energy

South – feminine energy

Spiral going clockwise – an outward journey connecting in the world

Spiral going counterclockwise – an inward journey connecting
within self

EARTH ELEMENTS AND SEASONS

Water – emotion

Air – logic and analytical thinking

Fire – passion and creativity

Rain – forgiveness

Wind – change

Earth – mother

Mountains – father

Sun – masculine

Moon – feminine

Sky – consciousness and masculinity

Sea or ocean – subconscious, femininity, emotion

Cliff – turning points or critical changes necessary
Spring – innocence and new beginnings
Summer – activity and action
Fall – learning lessons and harvest
Winter – physical healing and rest
The Five Elements with acupuncture meridians and corresponding
    emotions:

Fire	heart – shock, trauma and guilt	
	thyroid/adrenal – confusion	
	pituitary – unresponsive	
	small intestine – vulnerable	
Earth	stomach – disgust and despair	
	spleen/pancreas – low self-esteem, rejection	
Metal	lung – grief	
	large intestine – stuck	
Water	kidney – fear	
	bladder – irritated	
Wood	liver – anger	
	gallbladder – resentment	

FLOWERS

Apple blossom – hope and good fortune
Begonia – fanciful and whimsical
Bluebell – gratitude
Carnation – fidelity and deep love
Chrysanthemum – love and truth
Daffodil – regard and devotion
Daisy – innocence, youth, gentleness
Hibiscus – delicate beauty
Gardenia – awakening intuition
Iris – a message
Ivy – friendship and fidelity
Jasmine – grace and elegance
Jonquil – affection returned
Lavender – luck
Lilacs – first emotions of love
Lily – purity

Lily of the Valley – return to happiness
Marigold – affection
Mums – I love
Pansy – thinking of you, thoughtful recollection
Peony – bashfulness, healing
Rose – single rose means 'I love you', two roses to form a single stem means an engagement, stem leaves, a symbol of hope.
  Red rose – love and passion
  White Rose – purity and humility
  Pink Rose – grace and perfect happiness
  Yellow rose – joy and gladness
Sunflower – adoration
Tulip – love and passion
Verbena – enchantment
Violet – modesty and simplicity
Water lily – purity of heart
Zinnia – thoughts of absent friends

FOOD

Fruit – innocence and new beginnings
Vegetables – taking harvest and completion
Eggs – rebirth and opportunity
Meat – sacred energy of ritual and tribal strength
Fish – sacred energy of ritual and tribal wisdom
Milk – feminine nourishment
Breads and grains – symbol of physical healing
Wine – symbol of spiritual commitment
Sliced Carrots – look like the human eye, the pupil, iris and radial lines look like the human eye, eating carrots greatly enhances blood flow to and functions of the eye
Tomato – the heart has four chambers and is red like the tomato, and tomatoes are pure heart blood food
Grapes – hang in clusters like the heart, with each grape like a blood cell, and grapes are profound heart and blood vitalizing food
Walnut – looks like a brain, left and right hemisphere, upper and lower cerebellum, even the folds are like the neo-cortex, and walnuts enhance brain function

Kidney beans – actually heal and help maintain kidney functions

Celery, Bok Choy, Rhubarb – look like bones, these foods as well as bones are 23% sodium and are an excellent source to replenish skeletal needs of the body

Eggplant, Avocadoes and Pears – look like the womb and cervix and are a marvelous supplement for balancing hormones and preventing cervical cancer

Figs – are full of seeds and hang in twos when they grow, and are great to increase motility of male sperm and increase sperm to overcome sterility

Sweet Potatoes – look like the pancreas and actually balance the glycemic index of diabetics

Olives – assist the health and function of the ovaries

Grapefruit, oranges and other citrus fruits – look like the mammary glands and actually assist the health of the breast and the movement of lymph in and out of the breast

Onions – look like body cells and onions help clear waste materials from all of the body cells

GIFTS

Bracelet – sacred symbol of believing in a cause, knowing your truth

Book – symbol of wisdom and history

Car – symbol of self

Child or baby – new beginnings and re-birth

Demons and dragons – the disowned parts of self

Empty box – a powerful symbol of all there is, full potential of anything you want and need, pure abundance, true confidence and self-esteem

Money or coins – symbol of prosperity

Musical instrument – speaking your truth and being understood

Necklace – according to Carl Jung, it symbolizes belonging to a tribe

Picture or picture album – symbol of our ancestors, our heritage

Pin – it symbolizes the belonging to self; confidence, self-love, self-esteem

Purse or bag – lessons learned

Ring – symbol of a union between two people, or a union within self
Robe or garment – symbol of being honored
Sword – symbol of masculine energy
Tree – symbol of self – roots grounding into earth, with the trunk our support and the branches our connections with the world, and the leaves our full potential self
Vase – symbol of feminine energy
Watch or clock – symbol of divine timing, to begin an adventure
White light – surrounding by the protection of your creator

HOUSE

Living room – how we wish to be seen in the world
Dining room – how we nurture other people
Kitchen – how we nurture ourselves or how we were nurtured as a child
Bedroom – our sensuality and sexuality
Bathroom – our pride in our physical appearance and general maintenance of our body
Attic – memories from our past or our connections with a higher power
Basement – old, unresolved, repressed issues from past
Front yard – how we project ourselves to others
Back yard – parts of self we are not comfortable with or are ashamed of
Right side of house – our aspirations and hopes for the future – masculine energy
Left side of the house – our past and how it affects us today – feminine energy

INSECTS

Ants – industriousness, order and discipline
Bees – fertility and the honey of life
Beetle – resurrection
Butterfly – transmutation and the dance of joy
Dragonfly – the power of light

Grasshopper – uncanny leaps forward
Praying mantis – power of stillness
Spider – creativity and the weaving of fate

NUMBERS

0 – all things are possible, the beginning
1 – an idea or thought
2 – gathering and learning
3 – the creation, the building
4 – the testing, the challenge
5 – the problem, something is broken
6 – the fixing and changing
7 – the sacred completion
8 – the sharing and worldly abundance
9 – the ultimate cycle, everything
10 – the beginning again

PLACES OF PEACE

Desert – the connection to ancient truth and wisdom
Fairyland of make believe – place of pure physical healing
Galaxy – strong connection to spirituality
Meadow – center place of connection, peace and calm, the larger
the meadow the more inner peace
Mountains – connection to the masculine strengths
Ocean – connection to the feminine strengths
Prairie and open fields – place of physical nourishment
Woods – connection to the deeper levels of our subconscious

REPTILES

Alligators and crocodiles – primal energies of birth, motherhood
and initiation
Chameleon – clairvoyance and psychic sensitivity
Frogs – transformation through water and sound
Lizards – subtlety of perception
Snake – rebirth, resurrection, initiation, and wisdom

Turtle – motherhood, longevity, awakening to opportunities

SHAPES

Circle – represents our solar plexus, our sense of wholeness, center of self-love, confidence and self-esteem.

Square – represents our connection to earth and grounding, our place of stability and security, usually associated with the first, second and third chakras

Triangle – represents our visions, goals and dreams, associated with the sixth chakra, the mystic third eye

Spiral – represents all change and growth happening in our life, correlated with the seventh chakra

Cross – our connection to others, our relationships, whether they are friends, lovers, family, associated with the throat chakra, that place of communicating and sharing our truth with others

SYMPTOMS AND PHYSICAL PROBLEMS

Symptoms are a marvelous way of listening to the body. The problem can be a message of what needs to be examined in our life, in our way of thinking, in our attitude. The body carries muscle memory, and often, the physical problem can be the beginning of letting go of old traumas or memories from the past. Below are excerpts from Louise L. Hay's book, *You Can Heal Your Life*, as well as *Feelings Buried Alive Never Die*, by Karol Truman.

In looking up any symptom or physical problem for yourself or your client, please bear in mind, the following interpretations are merely suggestions of possible meanings and clues of what the body may be trying to tell us. Never define a person by their disease and symptom. In imagery, having a dialogue with an animal that represents the pain or imbalance can be a marvelous springboard to finding resolution and healing. The possible metaphors below could provide some possible probative questions to ask the animal along the way.

Aches – longing for love, longing to be held

Addictions - running from the self, fear, not knowing how to love the self

Adrenal problems – defeatism, no longer caring for the self

AIDS – denial of the self, sexual guilt, a strong belief in not being good enough

Alcoholism – feelings of futility, guilt, inadequacy

Allergies – denying your own power

Alzheimer's – a desire to leave the planet, the inability to face life as it is

Amnesia – fear, running from life, inability to stand up for self

Ankle – represents mobility and direction

Anorexia – denying the self life, extreme fear, self-hatred and rejection

Anxiety – not trusting the flow and the process of life

Appetite Excessive – fear, needing protection, judging the emotions

Appetite Loss – fear, protecting the self, not trusting self

Arms – represent the capacity and ability to hold the experiences of life

Arthritis – feeling unloved, criticism, resentment

Asthma – searching for mother love. Inability to breathe for one's self, feeling stifled, suppressed crying

Back Problems

> Upper – lack of emotional support, feeling unloved, and holding back love

> Middle – guilt, stuck in all that stuff back there, get off my back

> Lower – fear of money, lack of financial support

Bladder Problems – anxiety, holding on to old ideas, fear of letting go, being pissed off

Bleeding – joy running out, anger

Blood – represents joy in the body, flowing freely

Blood problems – lack of joy, lack of circulation of ideas

Blood Pressure

> High – longstanding emotional problem not solved

> Low – lack of love as a child, defeatism

Bones – represents the structure of the universe

Brain – represents the computer, the switchboard

Breasts – represent mothering and nurturing

Breast Problems, Cysts, Lumps and Soreness – over-mothering, over-protection, over-bearing attitudes, cutting off nourishment

Breast Problems – fear or refusal to take in life fully, not feeling the right to take up space or even to exist at times

Bruises – the little bumps in life, self-punishment

Cancer – deep hurt, longstanding resentment, deep secret or grief eating away at the self, carrying hatreds, difficulty in moving forward, fear of choosing your own direction

Constipation – refusing to release old ideas, stuck in the past

Crying – tears are the river of life, shed in joy as well as in sadness and fear

Cystic Fibrosis – a thick belief that life won't work for you

Deafness – rejection, stubbornness, isolation

Diabetes – longing for what might have been, a great need to control, deep sorrow, no sweetness left

Diarrhea – fear, rejection, running off

Earache – anger, not wanting to hear, too much turmoil, parents arguing

Elbow – represents changing directions and accepting new experiences

Eye Problems – not liking what you see in your own life

>Astigmatism – fear of really seeing the self

>Cataracts – inability to see ahead with joy, dark future

>Children – not wanting to see what is going on in the family

>Crossed – not wanting to see what's out there, crossed purposes

>Farsighted – fear of the present

>Glaucoma – stony inability to forgiveness, pressure from long-standing hurts, overwhelmed by it all

>Near sightedness – fear of the future

Face – represents what we show the world

Fatigue – resistance, boredom, lack of love for what one does

Feet – represent our understanding of ourselves, of others

Female Problems – denial of the self, rejecting femininity, rejection of the feminine principle

Fingers – represent the details of life

Thumb – represents intellect and worry
Index Finger – represents ego and fear
Middle Finger – represents anger and sexuality
Ring Finger – represents unions and grief
Little Finger – represents the family and pretending
Foot Problems – fear of the future and of not stepping forward in life
Gas Pains – fear, undigested ideas
Gastritis – prolonged uncertainty, a feeling of doom
Genitals – represent the masculine and feminine principles
     Problems – Worry about not being good enough
Gum Problems – inability to back up decisions, wishy-washy about life
Hands – hold and handle, grasping and letting go, all ways of dealing with experiences
Hay Fever – emotional congestion, a belief in persecution, guilt
Headaches – invalidating the self, self-criticism, fear
Heartburn – clutching fear
Heart – represents the center of love and security
     Problems – longstanding emotional problems, lack of joy
Hernia – ruptured relationships, strain, burdens, incorrect creative expression
Hip – carries the body in perfect balance, major thrust in moving forward
Hip Problems – fear of going forward in major decisions, nothing to move forward to
Indigestion – gut-level fear, dread, anxiety, griping and grudging
Infection – irritation, anger, annoyance
Insomnia – fear, not trusting the process of life, guilt
Itching – desires that go against the grain, unsatisfied, remorse, itching to get out or get away
Jaw Problems – anger, resentment, desire for revenge
Joints – represent changes in direction in life and the ease of these movements
Kidney Problems – criticism, disappointment, failure, shame, reacting like a little kid
Knee – represents pride and ego

Problems – stubborn ego and pride, inability to bend, inflexibility

Legs – carry us forward in life

Upper leg problems – holding on to old childhood traumas

Lower leg problems – fear of the future, not wanting to move

Leukemia – brutally killing inspiration

Liver – seat of anger and primitive emotions

Problems – chronic complaining, justifying fault-finding to deceive yourself, feeling bad

Lump in Throat – fear, not trusting the process of life

Lung – the ability to take in life

Problems – depression, grief, fear of taking in life, not worthy of living fully

Lupus – giving up, better to die than stand up for one's self, anger and punishment

Menopause Problems – fear of no longer being wanted, fear of aging, not being good enough

Menstrual Problems – rejection of one's femininity, guilt, fear, belief that the genitals are sinful or dirty

Migraine Headaches – dislike against being driven, resisting the flow of life, sexual fears

Multiple Sclerosis – mental hardness, hard-heartedness, iron will

Muscular Dystrophy – extreme fear, frantic desire to control everything and everyone, a deep need to feel safe, loss of faith and trust

Nails – represent protection

Nail Biting – frustration, eating away at the self

Nausea – fear, rejecting an idea or experience

Neck – represents flexibility, the ability to see what's back there

Problems – refusing to see other sides of a question, stubbornness, inflexibility

Nervousness – fear, anxiety, struggle, rushing, not trusting the process of life

Nose – represents self-recognition

Nose Bleeds – a need for recognition, feeling unrecognized and unnoticed, crying for love

Ovaries – represent points of creation, creativity

Overweight – fear, need for protection, running away from feelings, insecurity, self-rejection, seeking fulfillment

Pain – guilt, guilt always seeks punishment

Pancreas – represents the sweetness of life

Parkinson's Disease – fear and an intense desire to control everything and everyone

Pneumonia – desperate, tired of life, emotional wounds that are not allowed to heal

Pre-Menstrual Syndrome – allowing confusion to reign, giving power to outside influences, rejection of the feminine processes

Prostate – represents the masculine principle

>Problems – mental fears weaken the masculinity, giving up, sexual pressure and guilt

Senility – returning to the so-called safety of childhood, demanding care and attention, a form of control of those around you, escapism

Shingles – waiting for the other shoe to drop, fear and tension, too sensitive

Shoulders – are meant to carry joy, not burdens

Sinus Problems – irritation to one person, someone close

Skin – protects our individuality

Skin Problems – anxiety, fear, old, buried stuff, I am being threatened

Slipped Disc – feeling totally unsupported by life, indecisive

Snoring – stubborn refusal to let go of old patterns

Spine – flexible support of life

Spinal curvature – the inability to flow with the support of life, fear and trying to hold on to old ideas, not trusting life, lack of integrity, no courage of convictions

Spleen – being obsessed about things

Sterility – fear and resistance to the process of life or not needing to go through the parenting experience

Stiffness – rigid, stiff thinking

Stomach – holds nourishment, digests ideas

> Problems – dread, fear of the new, inability to assimilate the new

Stroke – giving up, resistance, rather die than change, rejection of life

Stuttering – insecurity, lack of self-expression, not being allowed to cry

Swelling – being stuck in thinking, clogged, painful ideas

Teeth – represent decisions

> Problems – longstanding indecisiveness, inability to break down ideas for analysis and decisions

Testicles – masculine principle, masculinity

Throat – avenue of expression, channel of creativity

> Problems – the inability to speak up for one's self, swallowed anger, stifled creativity, refusal to change

Thymus – master gland of the immune system, feeling attacked by life

Thyroid – humiliation, I never get to do what I want to do

Tinnitus – refusal to listen, not hearing the inner voice

Toes – represent the minor details of the future

Tonsillitis – fear, repressed emotions, stifled creativity

Tumors – nursing old hurts and shocks, building remorse

Ulcers – fear, a strong belief that you are not good enough

Urinary Infections – anger, usually at the opposite sex or a lover, blaming others

Uterus – represents the home of creativity

Varicose Veins – standing in a situation you hate, discouragement, feeling overworked and overburdened

Venereal Disease – sexual guilt, need for punishment, belief that the genitals are sinful or dirty, abusing another

Warts – little expressions of hate, belief in ugliness

Wisdom Tooth Impacted – not giving mental space to create a firm foundation

Wrist – represents movement and ease, grace of connecting with others

Made in the USA
Lexington, KY
27 March 2015